D0127428

KATE'S STYLE

First edition for North America published in 2013
by Barron's Educational Series, Inc.

Text and Design © Carlton Books Limited 2013

All inquiries should be addressed to:
Barron's Educational Series, Inc.
250 Wireless Boulevard
Hauppauge, NY 11788
www.barronseduc.com

ISBN: 978-1-4380-0329-0

Library of Congress Control No: 2013931285

First published by Carlton Books Limited
20 Mortimer Street
London W1T 3JW

Senior Executive Editor: Lisa Dyer
Managing Art Director: Lucy Coley
Production Manager: Maria Petalidou
Copy Editor: Jane Donovan
Research assistant: Ellen Wallwork

Printed in China

9 8 7 6 5 4 3 2 1

KATE'S

Smart, Chic Fashion from a Royal Role Model

STYLE

CAROLINE JONES

BARRON'S

Contents

Introduction

Even when she was plain old Kate, a pretty student who just happened to be dating Britain's most eligible bachelor, there was something about Miss Middleton that captured the world's imagination. Back in 2002, the 20-year-old already possessed a certain quiet poise, along with an easy smile and an indisputable eye for a striking outfit. As Catherine, Duchess of Cambridge, the fresh-faced student has now evolved into a bona-fide fashion queen, with a wardrobe that has inspired millions of avid followers and has spawned a thousand imitations.

Part of the fascination is rooted in Kate's own history. The daughter of two former British Airways flight attendants, who went on to marry a prince and become a style icon, is perhaps as close to a modern-day fairytale as you can get. Her down-to-earth background has never prevented her from mingling effortlessly in elite circles, and it is this unique melting pot of middle- and upper-class influences that gave birth to her signature style—a perfect blend of chain store and designer clothing. Kate has mixed everything up to create a fresh twist on classic British clothing—a look so simple yet so stylish that women across the globe want to emulate it. It has turned the Duchess into a global trendsetter, with a host of blogs and Twitter feeds dedicated solely to hunting down her latest must-have outfit.

On April 29, 2011, that outfit was an incomparable Sarah Burton for Alexander McQueen wedding dress, but it's perhaps the smart choices she has made since that show-stopping day that have done more to cement Kate's fashion-leader credentials. In recent years, we have seen her consistently hone and perfect her personal style during a nonstop calendar of official engagements. Particular fashion highlights have included the stunning outfits she wore for the Diamond Jubilee celebrations and the London 2012 Olympics, but many of her more dressed-down casual looks have proved equally influential.

Selecting outfit after stunning outfit for such a variety of engagements on such a public stage is an enormously tricky task, but one that Kate pulls off with aplomb and without the assistance of so much as a personal stylist. If she can do all this on her own, then there's hope for the rest of us! And that's exactly why we've created this book—an insider's guide that not only celebrates Kate's inspirational fashion flair, but also makes it possible to steal some of her style tricks.

We begin by looking at the components of Kate's "look" and the impact it has had on both the retail and the fashion worlds. After that, the heart of the book focuses on what everyone wants to know most of all: Where exactly do the Duchess's key fashion pieces come from, and how can we follow her fashion lead without having to marry a prince or go bankrupt in the process? With beautiful glossy photographs, we break down 40 of Kate's most memorable outfits, examining the stores, the designers, and the history behind them.

Aside from revealing Kate's personal style secrets, the text is also packed with practical tips that hold true for any budget, such as how to pick the perfect "Kate" blazer, and ways to work her favorite nude heels. In short, it's everything you need to know to emulate perhaps the most stylish woman of the century: Catherine, Duchess of Cambridge, aka "Kate the Great."

All about Kate

In the ten years since she first caught Prince William's eye while wearing see-through chiffon at the now infamous University of St. Andrews student fashion show, Catherine, Duchess of Cambridge, has become one of the biggest British style icons in living memory. Her elegant look has sparked copycat imitations all over the world and has created a recession-beating boost in sales for the stores and designers whose clothes she favors. Indeed, so pronounced is the "Kate Effect" globally that, in 2012, *Time* magazine selected Kate as one of the 100 Most Influential People in the World.

Kate's sartorial superstar status was cemented a year earlier when she was crowned the "Queen of Style" by upscale fashion bible *Harper's Bazaar*. In topping the magazine's celebrated Britain's Best Dressed list, Kate was praised for her "effortless" mix of high-end and chain store style, as well as for her role in the "fashion moment of the century"—her Sarah Burton for Alexander McQueen wedding dress. This was the making of a modern princess, played out in her fashion choices—as *Harper's* editor Lucy Yeomans noted: "Catherine's incredible style evolution has gripped us all."

RIGHT: Kate wore this glamorous floor-length coral satin dress by designer Issa to attend the Boodle Boxing Ball in aid of the Starlight Children's foundation at the Royal Lancashire Hotel London on January 7, 2008.

OPPOSITE: The Duchess wears a pretty floral dress by Jenny Packham to a charity polo match in Santa Barbara on July 9, 2011, which she attended with husband Prince William.

The Evolution of an Iconic Look

After graduating from the University of St. Andrews in 2006 with an Art History degree, Kate worked as an accessories buyer for the British chain store Jigsaw. It was here, working behind the scenes, that she honed an ability to make classic chain store staples look like a million dollars and developed an eye for picking a simple but stunning final touch for an outfit—be it that perfect-width belt or eye-catching scarf. During her time there, Kate even collaborated with successful jewelry designer Claudia Bradby on a "coffee bean" necklace that became a bestseller.

And yet, as far back as 2002, when Kate first began dating Prince William, it was clear that the young lady knew how to dress. Despite her slightly shy public demeanor, Kate always had a firm idea of who she was, and she wasn't the type to be easily swayed by passing fashion fads.

Tall and slender, her model-like figure has always meant she could pull off pretty much any style or shape of clothing, so it's testament to her strong sense of identity that she has chosen, by and large, to stick to a simple but effective fashion formula. The look may have been honed, sharpened, and sprinkled with designer pieces over the last few years, but the fundamentals have been in place since her student days. Kate's fail-safe ensemble usually includes: knee-length shift dresses, simple pumps, and her favorite envelope-style clutch purse. These elegant shapes flatter her thin frame and have become the mainstay of her wardrobe. They also echo her character traits of loyalty, stability, and quiet confidence.

The roots of Kate's look can be found in "Sloane" style—a not-always complimentary slang term used to describe the trendy upper middle-class inhabitants of expensive areas of west London, such as Chelsea and Kensington. The future Duchess may have been brought up in rural Berkshire, but throughout her private schooling she mixed with these trendy types, and now, as perhaps the most famous resident of west London, she is the foremost ambassador for the modern Sloane look. A typical "uniform" for a so-called Sloane Ranger includes costly country casuals such as Barbour wax jackets, navy blazers, and Hunter Wellington boots—a look worn by most members of the British Royal Family!

But while her trademark style is not new, what makes Kate stand out is that she has added her very own modern twists to invigorate what was essentially a tired, out-of-touch look. If Sloane style is typically safe and slow to evolve, Kate has extended it to include innovative dresses by high-fashion designers, along with a good-sized helping of chain store flourishes. This embrace of the best of British retailers has been particularly important in fostering the public's love affair with the Duchess. It's safe to say that in these financially troubled times, much of the appeal of Kate's signature style is that it feels accessible.

OPPOSITE AND ABOVE: Sloane style outdoors: Kate at the Badminton Horse Trials in May 2007, opposite far left; at a game fair at Blenheim Palace in July 2004, opposite left; attending the Golden Metropolitan Polo Club Charity Cup polo match, in which Prince William and Prince Harry played, at the Beaufort Polo Club in June 2012.

OVERLEAF: Kate in night-out-on-the-town mode, both 2007.

Another notable aspect of Kate's look is her old-fashioned take on female sexuality. With skirts never too short and heels never too high, her style has been dubbed "the new demure" but she still manages to look feminine and alluring. Less is certainly more, as far as she is concerned. This focused, but not inflexible style is what has helped Kate assume iconic fashion status. Like any classic style idol—from Audrey Hepburn and her boyish Capri pants and ballet flats to Gwen Stefani and her rock glamour—it's all about finding a strong look and ensuring its themes run through every outfit you choose. With Kate, this strong style core seems to come naturally as she channels her sartorial heritage with charm, but manages to appear fresh and modern at the same time.

The fact that royal etiquette forbids the Duchess to accept freebies may have contributed to her independent thinking. Unlike your average celebrity, Kate is not married to any of the big fashion houses and simply wears clothes that she really likes. She probably even looks at the price tags! Her independent streak runs deep—in this day and age, it's hard to believe that Kate has never once hired a personal stylist. Instead, she has masterminded her own fashion transformation, single-handedly shopping for all her own clothes. This brave decision shows how much the Duchess knows her own mind and is an indication that she doesn't indiscriminately choose pieces, but is making a deliberate, well-thought-out style statement.

And the personal involvement shows—despite the international stage and media masses, Kate never looks like a clotheshorse wearing some uncomfortable creation for the first time. On almost all occasions, formal and informal, she appears relaxed, self-assured, and totally happy with her outfit choices. After all, this is a lady who is confident enough in her shopping skills to think nothing of paying a visit to the local shopping outlet to pick up a bargain-priced Missoni coat for an official engagement with HM the Queen!

Although Kate still gravitates toward the mid-range British chain stores such as Whistles, L.K. Bennett, and Reiss, as she has been increasingly thrust into the limelight, her style has continued to mature and evolve. With the confidence of an established public figure—not to mention the wedding ring on her finger—the Duchess is now increasingly experimenting and has become more playful with her outfits, choosing vibrant colors and eye-catching designs for evening wear, such as the striking Jenny Packham teal ballgown she wore to an Olympic gala in May 2012. She has also started to reach for more accessories to refresh her look and has become quite the accomplished hat wearer, as demonstrated by the stylish tan Whiteley Hat Company headpiece she wore to the Epsom Derby races in June 2011. Teamed with a white Reiss dress, Joseph jacket, and L.K. Bennett clutch, it triggered a flurry of sales, with U.K. department store Debenhams selling seven for every hat. And, in November 2012, she decided to reinvent the carefully blow-dried long hairstyle she had sported since her college days by adding daring side bangs.

The "Kate Effect"

It's safe to say that the Duchess's impact on hat sales wasn't an isolated case. Figures from search engine Google reveal that "Kate Middleton" is one of the most searched-for fashion buzzwords, as followers desperately try to find out where her latest outfit was purchased and how they can get their hands on it. She may rarely be seen wearing something as pricey as the latest must-have Manolo Blahniks or Mulberry tiger-print bag, but the Duchess certainly has the ability to sell thousands of copies of her chain store favorites, be it a simple Zara dress or a pair of L.K. Bennett pumps.

Kate is perhaps the first style superstar of the social media age, and her effect on sales is often instantaneous as her fans immediately take to Twitter and Facebook to find out more. Numerous blogs, including *What Kate Wore*, and mobile apps such as *Kate's Style List*, have been launched to make following her fashion choices even easier. Examples of this effect are everywhere. When Kate wore a black velvet coat by Libélula to the wedding of Sarah Stourton and Harry Aubrey-Fletcher in January 2011, it sold out in just hours, the company website crashed, and the coat soon had a waiting list of 300.

After Kate chose to wear a Reiss "Nannette" dress for her engagement portrait by Mario Testino, astonished company founder David Reiss stated: "We have been inundated with press coverage—at one stage, online was selling one per minute." The Duchess again opted for the chain store brand when she met the Obamas at Buckingham Palace during their visit in May 2011. Unsurprisingly, the "Shola" pale camel bandage dress she wore flew out of stores at rapid speed. "We're really proud that Kate is a Reiss customer," said a delighted David Reiss, with some understatement. "She has the eyes of the world on her and is an incredible ambassador."

Even a low-key engagement can have the same effect. When Kate chose to wear a red Luisa Spagnoli suit to visit her old university, St. Andrews, she caused a now-familiar shopping frenzy at Hollie de Keyser, the London boutique that stocks the label. "We re-ordered 100 suits—that's over $80,600-worth of stock. Since Kate wore the suit, we've been inundated," the store reported.

And if customers cannot always afford the real thing, simply buying something similar will often suffice. Perhaps unsurprisingly, the famous royal blue Issa dress, worn by Kate when Buckingham Palace announced the royal engagement, sold out in under 24 hours. More impressively, the copycat version at U.K. low-cost supermarket Tesco was also snapped up within an hour of going online. And after Kate's $1,000 Burberry coat quickly sold out after she first wore it in March 2011, George at Asda (the U.K.'s version of Walmart) quickly reported a 300 percent surge in sales of their similar bargain-priced trench.

Kate's fashion influence isn't just restricted to the general public. Hollywood's elite have been equally impressed by the

Duchess's dress sense, with super-stylish *Devil Wears Prada* actress Anne Hathaway speaking for many when she declared: "Can I tell you how grateful I am to Kate Middleton? Because she is such an advocate for dressing like a lady. . . So right now my fashion choices are all about Kate Middleton."

Even for a Queen-in-waiting, Kate's impact so far on the fashion industry has been truly remarkable, already surpassing that of her style icon predecessor, Diana, Princess of Wales. The impact is now so pronounced that any brand ailing in the current economy must hope and pray that the Duchess decides to slip on one of their designs. Time and again we have seen her endorsement of certain labels cause shoppers to forget the recession and spend, spend, spend! In fact, when you start to do the math, the "Kate Effect" is probably unparalleled in fashion history in terms of its impact on sales.

In 2012, the year that London hosted the Olympic Games, British newspaper the *Daily Mail* suggested that the "Kate Effect" could well have generated a $3 billion cash bonanza for Britain's ailing economy, and quoted Dr. Harold Goodwin, a professor of tourism at Leeds Metropolitan University, as saying: "I wouldn't be surprised if Kate Middleton's legacy is bigger than that of the Olympics, domestically and internationally."

OPPOSITE: Kate holds her own in a simple camel bandage "Shola" dress from one of her favorite brands, Reiss, while meeting the equally stylish U.S. First Lady Michelle Obama at Buckingham Palace on May 24, 2011.

ABOVE: Kate cheers on the British Olympic team at the Women's Laser Radial race in Weymouth in August 2012, along with Princess Anne and Sir Steve Redgrave.

Pippa: It's a Sister Act

Of course, Kate isn't the only Middleton lady to have hit the style headlines. Ever since younger sister Pippa assisted Kate down the aisle at Westminster Abbey, she's been creating some fashion waves of her own. Her stunning yet simple cream silk Alexander McQueen bridesmaid dress drew praise from around the world—much of it centered on her well-shaped figure, gaining the then-27-year-old the press nickname "Her Royal Hotness."

But it's not just her derrière that has caused excitement—her sense of style has created its own "Pippa Effect" on clothes sales. This phenomenon first started when the Zara jacket she wore on her first public outing after the Royal Wedding became an instant classic. Soon after, her trusty Modalu "Bristol" bag was quickly renamed the "Pippa," and U.K. store John Lewis was crediting Kate's sister for helping them ride out their sales slumps.

Pippa's style, it must be said, is heavily indebted to her older sister, as demonstrated by the fact that, when she attended the wedding of Camilla Hook to Sam Holland in May 2012, she wore a red version of the same Issa "Forever" dress that Kate famously wore in her royal engagement photos. And yet, as befits a younger sister, Pippa does have a noticeable penchant for brighter colors and higher hemlines. It's a more overtly sexy style that suits her unmarried status—and also reflects the fact she's not set to be a future queen! But like her royal sibling, Pippa continues to loudly declare her love of retailers by stepping out in bargain dresses and jackets. When she attended the U.S. Open Tennis Championships on her 29th birthday in September 2012, she wore a canary-yellow shift dress by Phase Eight—a mid-price, chain store brand specializing in day and formal dresses. On the same trip, she worked both a bold multicolored block dress by London designer Paper, and a sky-blue blouse from ubiquitous chain store brand Next. Perhaps unsurprisingly, Pippa's unofficial visit to the States was attracting the attention of some serious players in the U.S. fashion world.

Kate Spade New York spoke for many when it commended Pippa on her "feminine yet modern sense of style," noting: "She always looks effortlessly put together and isn't afraid to wear color." The same label were also impressed by Pippa's take on a great Middleton tradition: fashion recycling. "We think it's fantastic how Pippa repeats her outfits and accessories," said a spokesperson for Kate Spade. "It sets a great example that fashion doesn't have to be thrown out after one wear." With such global style recognition, little wonder Pippa was also named by *Time* magazine as one of their 100 Most Influential People of 2012—a new entry that ousted poor Prince William from the list!

But it was in October 2012, at the launch of her party book *Celebrate: A Year of British Festivities for Families and Friends*

OPPOSITE AND ABOVE:
Pretty girls in pretty dresses. Kate and Pippa attend Simon Sebag Montefiore's *Young Stalin* book launch on May 14, 2007, at Aspreys, London, opposite, and the sisters walk around town in 2008, above.

that Pippa really sealed her fashion status in the eyes of the world. Ms. Middleton wore no fewer than four different designer dresses over 24 hours in London—costing a total of around $4,800. She began her day with a visit to Foyles bookstore for her first signing, wearing a "Vespa" patchwork dress by Paper London, then headed off to Daunt Books in Chelsea, finding time for a dress and hair change on the way. She arrived in a purple Roksanda Ilincic "Ayden" dress in wool-crepe, with her hair styled in a half-up, half-down do, very reminiscent of the Duchess of Cambridge. Minutes later, Pippa had changed into a black and green dress by hip fashion designer Markus Lupfer to throw a children's Halloween party. Afterward, she dashed off for her final costume change, reappearing at her evening event in the pièce de resistance: a tweed and black Stella McCartney dress. An exhausting but highly stylish day created a complete shopping frenzy as Pippa fans tried to buy at least one of her gorgeous frocks the following day.

As Pippa continues to be seen in front-row seats at some of the hottest designer fashion shows in London and New York, and has the freedom to wear edgier outfits than her royal sister, some observers speculate that her sense of style will continue to grow, and she may even land a role of her own in the fashion industry.

Carole: the Fashion-forward Mom

With two famously fashionable daughters, mom Carole was never going to escape intense style scrutiny but, thankfully for Mrs Middleton, in her role as family matriarch, she cuts an effortlessly elegant figure at every occasion. In fact, with her careful choice of well-cut beautiful garments, Carole has quickly become a flag-bearer for chic, age-appropriate attire, making it crystal-clear where Kate and Pippa inherited their taste and knack for show-stopping outfits.

Like her daughters, Carole chose wisely for the Royal Wedding, sporting a pale blue, wool-crepe coatdress by Catherine Walker that was a triumph of understated charm. Anxious not to take the spotlight away from her eldest daughter, mom managed to look modern without appearing to try too hard, while still conforming to the conventions of old-school British formal occasion dressing. It came as no surprise, then, that both the Walker ensemble and the equally well-received Gérard Darel suit she wore the following day sold out immediately.

OPPOSITE: Jeans and blazers in London's King's Road. Kate and Pippa Middleton go shopping in July 2007.

BELOW: Mother-and-daugher style: Kate Middleton and her mother Carole visit the "Spirit of Christmas Shopping" festival at London's Olympia exhibition hall in 2005. Kate's classic Chanel-style tweed blazer smartens up her faded blue jeans.

Carole does, in fact, have some experience in the world of fashion retail, which may provide a little insight into her style savvy. Aside from setting up her own successful party supplies mail-order company, Party Pieces, she has used her creative flair to help design the website for retail clothes chain Jigsaw's "Junior" line. Nevertheless, having the aplomb to dress your age, and well, is an impressive feat and one that Carole has pulled off time and again. Even when sporting a plunging, black V-neck gown at the Royal Wedding evening reception at Buckingham Palace, she managed to look alluring rather than vulgar.

Her beauty and sense of style have not gone unnoticed by those in the fashion world, with designer Karl Lagerfeld commenting in 2012: "I think Carole is very sexy. There is something full of life about her. For a woman who must be 50 or so, I think she's great. Full of energy."

These days, Carole Middleton is even following in the footsteps of both her daughters as the inspiration for a new collection of clothing based on her wardrobe. The clothing line was created in 2012 for George at Asda after customers said they desperately wanted to emulate Mrs. Middleton's style. George's brand director, Fiona Lambert, explained the appeal: "Carole Middleton is someone who always really gets it right for her age. She's elegant and stylish, but with a fashion-forward edge."

Kate the Great

Like her fashion-forward mother and style-conscious younger sibling, and even without her royal title, Catherine Elizabeth Middleton would no doubt have grown into an excellent shopper and a stylish dresser. She may even have become a minor trendsetter working within the fashion industry. But it is Kate's fate to, one day, become Queen, a singular destiny that sets her apart from those in the fashion world, including her own mother and sister. And yet if all the expectation and attention are a burden, the Duchess wears it as she does every other item in her wardrobe—with an elegant ease and a supreme confidence. As she is certain to continue evolving as a style icon for many years to come, we can only remark how lucky we are to have Kate as the current and future Queen of Style.

RIGHT: Kate and her family attend the Sovereign's Parade on December 15, 2006, at the Royal Military Academy in Sandhurst.

Kate's Calendar of Style

LEFT TO RIGHT: The young couple at the University of St. Andrews, June 2005; Kate modeling the Charlotte Todd transparent dress at the St. Andrews Fashion Show, March 2002; Graduation Day, June 2005; Biking to the gym, July 2005; Participating in the Sisterhood rowing team, August 2007; At the Mahiki nightclub, February 2007; Skiing in Klosters, Switzerland, March 2008.

LEFT TO RIGHT: Channeling sexy '70s style at the Day-Glo Midnight Roller Disco Charity, September 2008; Attending the Diamond Jubilee Tour, Solomon Islands, September 2012; Elegant at Wimbledon in July 2012; Cheering on at the Olympics in August 2012.

NEXT SPREAD: Unforgettable bridal attire, both by Sarah Burton for Alexander McQueen, the Royal Wedding, April 29, 2011.

The Look Book

The style evolution of Kate Middleton into a modern royal role model has gripped fashion fans across the globe. In the February 2013 issue, to celebrate Kate's 31st birthday, the British edition of *Vogue* magazine undertook an encyclopedic-like look at her dress sense, named Katepedia, an honor bestowed by the magazine only once before—on her grandmother-in-law, the Queen.

Among other things, *Vogue*'s number-crunching discovered that blue is by far Kate's preferred fashion color, with the Duchess wearing it 24 percent of the time for official occasions, while a clutch purse is her go-to accessory, with Kate carrying it to over 90 percent of engagements. The glossy also noted that Kate opted for outfits with a boatneck a little over 40 percent of the time.

In a similar spirit of admiration and with equally careful attention to detail, we take a forensic look at Kate's most seminal outfits, examining the key looks that helped create a global style queen. From the chic navy lace and nude silk Erdem dress she wore as part of the royal couple's official tour of Canada and North America, to the stunning Alice Temperley black lace evening gown she has recycled on two occasions, the Duchess of Cambridge's sartorial selections have sent both lower-end brands and designer sales soaring as fans try to emulate her impeccable ladylike style.

Whether dressed down in an L.K. Bennett sheepskin coat, jeans, and Le Chameau wellies to watch Prince William play in a soccer match, or wowing the crowds in a formal Alexander McQueen scarlet suit during the Queen's Diamond Jubilee pageant, Kate's clothing choices are consistently classic, well considered, and elegant.

On nearly every occasion, Kate's outfits reward closer examination. Indeed, the close inspection we offer here merely mirrors Kate's own attention to detail. On official tours of both Canada and the South Pacific and Far East, she has carefully sought out local designers to give a stylish nod to her host, like when she wore a striking purple and cream floral silk dress by Singaporean-born designer Prabal Gurung to attend a state dinner in Singapore. On other occasions, Kate has even displayed a cute sense of humor, making insider jokes only fashionistas would catch, such as the shoes named after a type of daffodil, the Welsh national flower, which she wore on the Welsh national holiday, St. David's Day.

It is both this classic, affordable chic and the subtle personal touches that make a journey through Kate's key looks so inspirational and rewarding. Read on to discover how a pretty girl named Kate, without so much as a stylist to guide her, became a Duchess that dazzled the world.

Shopping Spree Chic

The Dress When Kate decided to do some last-minute honeymoon shopping on April 20, 2011—just nine days before her wedding to Prince William—she knew the eyes of the world's press would be upon her. So she chose a fittingly restrained yet stylish black wrap-dress for her trip to King's Road in London's Chelsea—a street that has been synonymous with fashion since its heyday during the Swinging Sixties.

The bride-to-be turned to one of her most trusted labels, Issa, for this key shopping expedition, choosing a casual design with short sleeves, a deep V-neckline, and gathered detail at the waist and shoulders. The 100 percent silk frock hit all the right style notes and ensured she looked sexy yet demure as she strode between stores. And in defying the old adage that royals should only wear black if someone has died, she also demonstrated how she has quietly put her own stamp on Britain's most formal family when it comes to outfit etiquette.

As for Kate's trip—it ended up turning into quite a spree, with the bride-to-be buying several items from U.K. chain stores Warehouse and Whistles, as well as Banana Republic, which she is said to love, as they offer exactly the kind of sleek, fuss-free wardrobe staples she wears so well.

The Shoes Kate accessorized her outfit with a familiar pair of tan kitten-heeled, pointed-toed shoes with a gold buckle. These particular favorites are designed by Italian label Salvatore Ferragamo, whose unique style of handmade leather shoes are coveted around the world. Founder Ferragamo died in 1960 but during his heyday the Naples-born shoemaker famously worked with many style icons, including Eva Peron and Marilyn Monroe, and his label remains the go-to brand for stylish celebrities from Kate Moss to Carey Mulligan.

The Bag Kate teamed her heels with a Prada bowling bag in a matching shade, with her contrast of tan and black proving once more that she is not afraid to break a few established fashion rules and add a modern edge to classic outfits.

The Jewelry With her wedding just days away, the only jewelry Kate needed to accessorize her outfit was her 18-carat sapphire and diamond engagement ring—a piece that previously belonged to Diana, Princess of Wales. The elegant cluster ring from royal jeweler Garrard sent a clear message so onlookers were left in no doubt exactly which family she was about to marry into!

Stay Unruffled as You Shop

Shopping at the mall, racing in and out of different stores to try on a host of new outfits, can leave even the coolest fashionista looking distinctly disheveled. And more, Kate knows that even on the most mundane of trips, she is bound to be snapped by a raft of photographers. This has made it doubly important for the Duchess to simplify and refine a workable "day at the stores" look. As always, Kate doesn't disappoint by sticking to a few style-savvy rules.

Pick a dress with easy access!

Kate's choice of a wrap dress is perfect for clothes shopping. Because it opens at the front, it can be put on and taken off quickly, allowing her to try things on without disturbing her hair and makeup or getting makeup on clothes. This ensures her groomed look is maintained from store to store and that she is not unwittingly snapped looking windswept.

Opt for mid-heels

Kitten heels such as Kate's Ferragamos are an ideal compromise for shopping—they offer more comfort than high heels but are still more glamorous than flats, so she cuts an elegant figure.

Keep hair easy-to-wear

An up-do is a no-no when trying on clothes, as it will soon be disturbed and end up looking messy by the time you're finished. Kate cleverly opts for a simple blow-out, finished off with pretty tousled curls, which means a quick shake after each clothing change, and her style looks as good as new.

Choose muted tones of makeup

A shopping session is not the time to try out a new bright lipstick or strong shade of eyeshadow. Chances are you'll end up with nasty smears as you try on prospective purchases. Here, Kate keeps it simple with her trademark barely-there makeup consisting of just enough neutral eyeliner and lip gloss to look fresh and polished. No wonder her preferred makeup brand is Bobbi Brown—famed for its earthy tones and natural finish. Its makeup artist founder, Ms. Brown, explains the philosophy behind her products like this: "Women want to look and feel like themselves, only prettier and more confident. The secret to beauty is simple—be who you are."

How to Accessorize like Kate

Kate favors understated jewelry and a minimal color palette that allows the focus to be firmly centered on her dress and figure. Her sapphire and diamond engagement ring is such a scene-stealer that she ensures all her other pieces complement it rather than compete with it—this navy and nude ensemble perfectly mirrors her sapphire and gold jewelry.

Choose delicate, matching jewelry
Drop earrings and fine-chain necklaces and bracelets are Kate's usual go-to style, and she's abandoned the chunkier rings and heavy earrings from her single days. First seen on her engagement day, her Elsa Peretti "Cabochon by the Yard" necklace from Tiffany's is a simple 18-carat gold chain with a central lapis lazuli cabochon spaced with two round brilliant diamonds. It is often worn with a matching bracelet with three bezel-set diamonds separated by a chain, from Tiffany's "Diamonds by the Yard" collection. Lapis lazuli cabochon drop earrings, set in yellow gold bezel and hanging from a bezel-set diamond stud (see facing page), complement her engagement ring.

Matching your shoes, hat, and bag
The 1950s tradition of matching accessories is a style technique favored by Kate for keeping the whole ensemble tied together. Although indicative of a cautious approach to dressing, keeping to a two-color schematic, like Kate, does allow the whole look to be sleek, managed, and minimal. The essential factor to making this a successful look, however, is adding texture—mixing lace or silk with shiny patent leather, snakeskin, or raffia accessories.

LOOK 2

Nude and Navy, Kate's Classic Combination

The Dress Kate wore this stunning navy lace and nude "Cecile" dress for the first day of her Canadian tour in July 2011. During the seven-hour flight, Kate performed a flawless turnaround, changing into this eye-catching dress, which is designed by Erdem Moralioglu. The scoop-backed, shift dress contrasts stone crepe with a navy lace overlay and flashes a sheer lace sleeve with a scallop detail.

Not only was it a stylish choice, it was a diplomatic one, too. Erdem Moralioglu is based in London but was born in Canada, so it carefully references both nations. The designer is also hot fashion property, with fans including Samantha Cameron, Michelle Obama, and Gwyneth Paltrow, helping prove Kate can do high-fashion as well as retail. The Duchess's dress is from the designer's Resort 2012 collection.

The Bag Kate sticks to her faithful style of purse to carry with formal wear: the clutch. This nude animal-print version is from L.K. Bennett, and Kate's been snapped carrying it with many different outfits. And no wonder—its neutral tone means it works well with most colors.

The Shoes On Kate's feet were her much-loved cream L.K. Bennett "Sledge" shoes that she has worn on several recent public occasions. Predictably, the style soon sold out, both online and in-store, while pairs on eBay were going for nearly double the retail price.

Neutral shoes have definitely become de rigueur recently, with Kate the reigning queen of nude footwear. She relied heavily on the style for her first overseas tour of Canada, and has worn them at many other official engagements, teaming them with a variety of outfits. They are a very flattering choice, as not only do nude shoes elongate the leg, they go with everything, working particularly well as a foil for bold colors or strong prints.

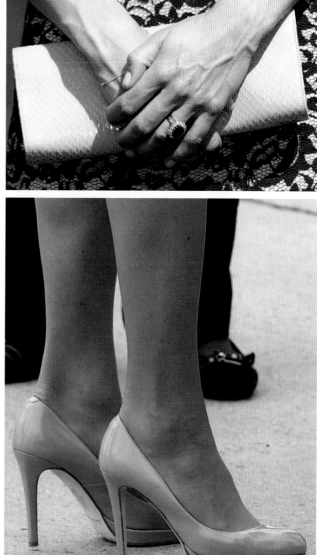

LOOK 3

Kate Recycles with Style

The Dress This white ruffled Reiss dress, chosen here by Kate for a ceremony in Ottawa during her royal tour of Canada in summer 2011, was the same frock she'd worn for her official engagement portrait with Prince William. The "Nanette" dress sold out almost immediately after Kate first wore it and had to be re-issued by the company, with the second release of inventory disappearing even faster than the original. The dress features three-quarter sleeves with a cascading frill down the front in a light chiffon fabric. British chain store Reiss is a firm favorite of Kate's, and its classic style with a modern twist suits her slender frame perfectly. It's not the first time the Duchess of Cambridge has worn a garment twice for public events— she makes a habit of re-wearing dresses she's worn previously, but usually updates the look with new accessories. The fact that she can successfully recycle old outfits makes Kate look both down-to-earth and confident in her sense of style.

OPPOSITE: This white ruffled Reiss dress Kate is wearing is a perfect example of the popular store's chic and stylish occasion-wear—and demonstrates why Kate so often relies on the brand for formal engagements that others might feel demanded a designer piece. The dress's simple lines are timeless, but the side frill and wrap-over skirt detail echo two key fashion trends of 2011, ensuring it is right on-trend.

The Hat This scarlet red felt, beret-style cap with flower embellishments is one of several hats made specifically for Kate's Canadian tour by her favorite milliner, Sylvia Fletcher at Lock & Co. Fletcher is known for creating eye-catching hats and headpieces that are worn by celebrities and royalty alike. The stylish hat also features Canada's national symbol, the maple leaf, as does her diamond brooch, which was borrowed from the Queen, who lent Kate a selection of pieces from her own personal jewelry collection for the Canadian tour—Kate's first official overseas engagement. By combining her white dress with red accessories, the Duchess is paying homage to the colors of Canada's national flag.

The Bag Kate's gorgeous scarlet and tan woven, fan-shaped clutch—from Anya Hindmarch's Spring/Summer 2011 collection —is a great finishing touch to her outfit and, like the hat, adds a dash of pretty detail and humor to an otherwise simple ensemble. Known for her quirky creations, British fashion accessories designer Hindmarch is a firm celebrity favorite, with fans that include Angelina Jolie, Scarlett Johansson, and Sienna Miller.

The Shoes The Duchess is always at her best when mixing chain store and designer accessories, as these vibrant red Albini square-cut pumps demonstrate perfectly.

Find Your Finishing Touches

After graduating from the University of St. Andrews in Scotland, Kate worked as an accessories buyer for Jigsaw, the popular British clothes chain that's known for mixing boho chic with classic tailoring. During her time there, she collaborated with the jewelry designer Claudia Bradby, and learned a lot about how to choose those all-important finishing touches. Here are some of her favorite tricks.

Get a good hair buddy

Great hair is a vital part of every ensemble, so it's worth spending time finding a hairdresser who understands your hair and how to get the best from it. Kate entrusts her shiny brunette locks to the Richard Ward Hair Salon just off Sloane Street in Chelsea, London. As well as performing regular trims, Richard styles Kate's hair for special occasions, which included her wedding.

Plump for pumps

Although she loves a high heel for formal occasions, Kate has figured out that the key to staying stylish while dressing casually is neat but classy footwear. Indeed, all of the Middleton women, Kate included, love French Sole—the brand best known for its elegant leather ballet flats.

Polished to Perfection

The Dress Kate dazzled in a regal purple Issa dress as the royal couple attended a concert to mark Canada Day on July 1, 2011. The snug-fitting gown boasted a shallow V-neck and was gathered in the front to accentuate Kate's enviably tiny waist.

Ever since Kate wore a blue Issa London wrap-dress to announce her engagement (see picture opposite), Brazilian-born Daniella Issa Helayel, the force behind Issa London, has designed a number of custom dresses especially for the Duchess. Helayel's designs are instantly recognizable and often feature her distinctive wrap-over shape. Issa dresses are made from a soft fluid silk jersey in a myriad of luminous colors. They often feature figure-flattering ruching and ruffles, creating garments that manage to be the right combination of classy, sexy, and comfortable. The Duchess of York's daughters, Princess Beatrice and Princess Eugenie, are also Issa fans.

The Bag Kate carried her black silk "Maud" clutch from the Anya Hindmarch Bespoke collection, which she first showcased when meeting the Obamas earlier that same year. The satiny soft bag is made of 100 percent silk thread woven to give a super-glossy appearance. Diana, Princess of Wales, also carried the "Maud" clutch, as has Carla Bruni-Sarkozy, Scarlett Johansson, and Kate Moss. Anya Hindmarch spoke of how happy she was that Kate chose one of her bags. "It is a real honor and I think she's an amazing pin-up for British fashion," Hindmarch said. "She's a beautiful girl. I love that she's not too 'high-fashion'."

The Brooch Proudly pinned to the Duchess's dress was a diamond, maple-leaf brooch that belonged to Queen Elizabeth, the Queen Mother, and that was given to the late monarch by the people of Canada in 1939. It was passed down to Kate's grandmother-in-law who wore it during her first visit to Canada in 1951. And this tradition was carried on as the Queen loaned it to Kate to wear on her first royal tour of the country in 2011.

The Shoes With her bright jewel-toned dress and eye-catching brooch, Kate kept the shoes simple, slipping into her trusted black Prada heels.

Perfect the Kate Up-do

Kate's go-to hairstyle is long glossy looks, loosely flowing around her shoulders. However, when she wants to make a hair statement, she often sweeps it back into a sleek chignon for a more polished look. Here's how to tame long locks into a chic chignon:

Separate hair into three sections
The first being midway to the ear, the second up to the crown of the head, and the third being the remaining strands at the back of your head.

Secure the bottom section into a ponytail
Tease the pony to create volume, then wrap it into a bun and secure it with bobby pins.

Split the second section of your hair (at the crown) into two with a diagonal part
Wrap these two pieces around the bun, with each going in an opposite direction.

Twist the front section of your hair
Wrap it around the chignon before pinning to secure. Finally, spritz with a strong-hold hairspray to keep your "do" in place.

LOOK 5

Kate's Understated Elegance

The Dress While attending a tree-planting ceremony during her Canadian tour, Kate wore this simple but oh-so-stylish metallic gray, short-sleeved, collared shift dress by one of Princess Diana's favorite designers, Catherine Walker. Some fashion critics slammed Kate's choice on this occasion as boring, but to do so is to miss the point of this timeless classic, which looks effortlessly elegant and perfectly accentuates her tiny waist.

The "Kensington" dress was also a very meaningful choice for Kate, as she has multiple family ties to the designer, who died last year after battling cancer. Princess Diana was an enormous fan of Ms. Walker's creations, and Kate's mother, Carole Middleton, wore a Catherine Walker ensemble for Kate and William's wedding in April 2011.

The Bag Kate loves a simple but elegant clutch purse, and not only does it look stylish, it's also perfect for giving her something to do with her hands when she's photographed. Plus, clutches have the benefit of not pulling on the shoulders and ruining the line of an outfit, as ordinary shoulder-strap purses often can. This silver-gray "Somerton" clutch is from Hobbs, another of her favorite chain stores, especially when it comes to their soft leather bags and shoes. Kate's teamed the look with a simple Links of London silver bracelet with ball detail, which shows off her slim wrists.

The Shoes These rather funky metallic snakeskin "Dela" pumps add a daring touch to an outfit that looks rather bland at first glance. The shoes are by breakout English-born designer Tabitha Simmons and are from her Fall/Winter 2011 collection. Ever since the Duchess was spotted in Simmons' creations, there has been a surge of interest in the model-turned-designer, who unveiled her super-slick debut shoe collection in 2009. Displaying Simmons' signature directional style, every pair of her shoes is handmade in Italy using the finest leather, and features intricate detailing and hidden platforms for extra height. The snakeskin adds interest and boldness to an otherwise clean-cut look.

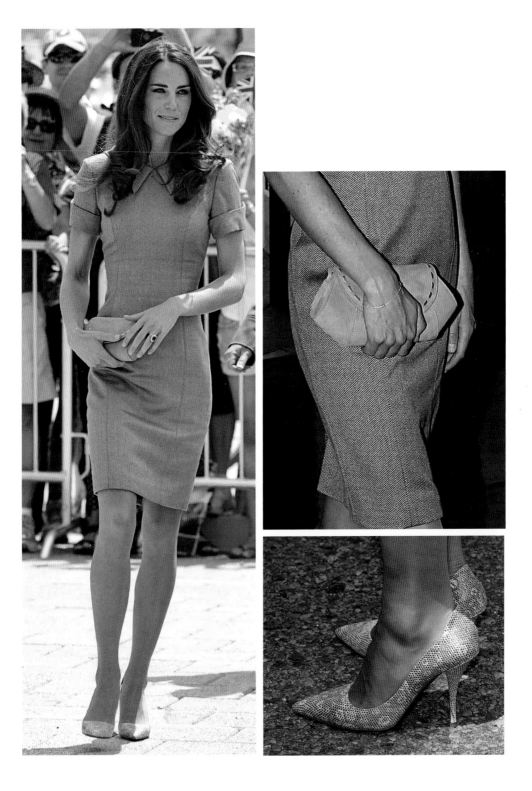

LOOK 6

Nautical Chic

The Dress Kate and William visited Charlottetown, the capital city of the Canadian province of Prince Edward Island (or "PEI," as it is known locally) on July 4, 2011. At a reception to welcome them to the island, she chatted excitedly about her childhood passion for the book *Anne of Green Gables*, which is set on PEI in 1878. The Duchess first read the classic novel by Canadian author Lucy Maud Montgomery when she was eight and she felt an affinity for the title character, Anne Shirley. Her love for the tale may have inspired her choice of dress that morning—as in the movie and television adaptation, the character of Anne often sported sailor-collar blouses and full skirts, similar in appearance to Kate's nautical-style, cream cable-knit sweater dress with navy piping around the cuffs and hem, and a silk collar with an anchor printed on it. The $1,780 long-sleeved dress was designed by none other than Sarah Burton for Alexander McQueen, the mastermind behind Kate's wedding dress. In wearing it, the Duchess proved she has an eye for timeless style and that she won't just blindly follow the latest fashion, as this piece was from the designer's 2006 collection.

OPPOSITE: Sarah Burton for Alexander McQueen has dressed Kate for no fewer than eight formal occasions, including in this sailor dress. Since taking the helm as creative director at McQueen following Alexander's death in 2010, Manchester-born Burton has impressively built on the label's considerable success. As a result, she was named Designer of the Year at the British Fashion Awards in November 2011, and included in *Time* magazine's annual list of the 100 most influential people in the world.

Revamp an Outfit You've Worn Before

As a true clothes lover, Kate likes to get good wear out of her favorite pieces. The Queen of Fashion Recycling knows how to prevent an often-worn outfit from looking tired. A year to the day after stepping out in this nautical dress and navy heels in Canada, Kate sported the very same outfit on a trip to Wimbledon's Royal Box. Here's how she kept it fresh:

Keep the setting in mind
The first time Kate wore this McQueen dress, she played up its nautical theme to pick up on PEI's fishing industry. However, the second time around it was the piece's similarity to Wimbledon tennis uniforms from the 1920s that she was referencing in her sartorial choice. Kate shrewdly realized that the two different settings would bring out two different stories from the same dress.

A change of hairstyle makes all the difference
At Wimbledon, Kate wore the dress with her hair cascading casually over her shoulders, rather than tied back in a loose ponytail, as she did at the more formal event the year before.

Be clever with accessories
The first time she wore the McQueen piece, Kate kept accessories to a minimum so all attention was focused on her dress. But at Wimbledon she paired it with a navy quilted Jaeger clutch, making an interesting fashion statement with the contrasting textures of bag and dress.

The Shoes Kate teamed her dress with simple blue suede classic heels from chain store L.K. Bennett, another of her favorite British brands. Its proprietor, Linda Kristin Bennett, was awarded an OBE for Services to the Fashion Industry in the 2006 New Year Honors list. Ms. Bennett is renowned for creating shoes that are both practical and glamorous. "When I set out, I wanted to produce something in-between the designer footwear you find in Bond Street and those on the high street," she explains. This makes her designs perfect for Kate, who is the Queen of Practical Glamour.

The Earrings Those diamond and sapphire cluster earrings were a gift from Prince William. They originally belonged to his late mother, Diana, Princess of Wales, and match Kate's engagement ring, which also once belonged to Diana. The earrings are thought to have been a wedding gift from the Crown Prince of Saudi Arabia, and Diana was spotted wearing them at dozens of events during the 1980s and 1990s. Kate put her own personal slant on the earrings and brought them into the twenty-first century by having the studs remodeled into drop earrings.

ABOVE LEFT AND RIGHT: The nautical look is a recurrent fashion theme for Kate, seen above left in a navy double-breasted Alexander McQueen military coat, worn in June 2011, and, above right, in a pencil skirt and blouse by McQueen, this time with sailor-inspired brass buttons, worn in August 2011.

LOOK 7

How Kate Wears Denim

The Jeans Kate certainly loves her J Brand 811 "Olympia" straight-leg jeans, wearing them three times on her summer 2011 Canadian tour with Prince William. She's also been seen sporting them on numerous other daytime occasions, and here is why: J Brand aren't just any jeans. Kate's discovered that their cut is pretty much the most flattering one available. No wonder the slim-fitting navy denims have become one of the fashion pack's must-have labels, with fans including Jessica Alba, Nicole Scherzinger, and Katie Holmes.

The Duchess no doubt loves that these jeans are free from obvious branding, but also for the fact that the luxe twill fabric is the perfect shade of inky navy blue and has just the right amount of stretch to flatter her shape.

American company J Brand was founded in 2004 and has soared in popularity over the past few years, thanks to their trend-led styles, such as the "Houlihan" cargo pants and "Love Story" flares.

The Belt This gorgeous chocolate-brown leather belt with brass buckle is by Kenya-based Linda Camm—an accessory designer who has become something of a cult buy and who has enjoyed a huge surge in sales since Kate wore her pieces in Canada. Camm's company is located in Tanzania, where she works with more than 200 Masai tribeswomen to create leather products with exquisite beadwork.

OPPOSITE: The J Brand jeans may have been the talking point when Kate wore this outfit to stroll around Slave Lake in Canada with Prince William in July 2011, but she also chose the occasion to debut what would become another favorite item—her preppy One-Button Blazer from the Canadian label Smythe. She has since worn this very versatile piece on numerous occasions, including several times during the London 2012 Olympic Games.

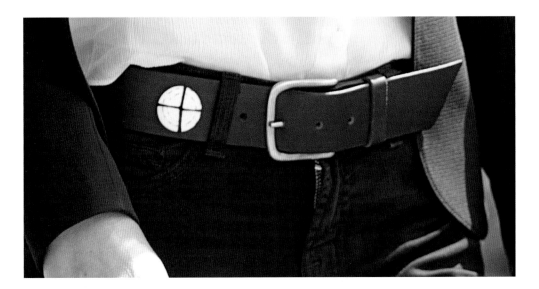

The Shoes Kate shows just how versatile her J Brand jeans are by dressing them up with a pair of black and woven straw L.K. Bennett "Maddox" wedges and navy Smythe blazer, and, later on the same day, working a more casual look with some suede taupe and white Sebago "Bala" moccasins—traditional boat shoes made in New England. Needless to say, after Kate wore them, the shoes, previously popular only in sailing circles, became hugely popular and sold out in the shade worn by the Duchess.

How to Make Blue Jeans Look Chic

As a true fashionista, Kate knows that you don't need a flashy, high-maintenance outfit to look stylish—a well-fitting, trendy pair of jeans can see you through most day-to-day situations. Here are a few tips on getting it right:

Pick the right shade
Kate's dark navy J Brands are the ultimate in versatile denim and can switch from casual to dressy with just a change of accessories.

Make sure your jeans fit
Kate's jeans are the perfect length and size for her frame. Poor-fitting denim looks cheap, not classy—and a designer name means nothing if your jeans are the wrong size or style for your body.

Go slim-cut, not skinny
Kate's figured out that, unless you're a rock star, super-skinny jeans can be just too darn tight to look elegant, so she opts for a slim or straight-leg cut instead. This makes her already-slim legs look even longer and works equally well with a casual checkered shirt and flats or a pretty fashion top and heels. Unless you want to look like a country-and-western singer, don't wear a matching denim jacket—wear a cotton jacket or blazer, like Kate.

Cowgirl Kate

The Shirt When Kate attended the Calgary Stampede, an annual Canadian festival celebrating the Western way of life, on July 8, 2011, she truly got into the spirit of the occasion in choosing this aptly named "Rodeo" shirt by Temperley London. Cut from a gossamer silk and cotton blend, the ivory shirt's sheer panels and delicate lace details soften the masculine silhouette of this Western look. The simple but stylish shirt from the British label's Pre-Fall 2011 collection was just one of many Temperley pieces that Kate chose to wear to accompany Prince William on the royal tour of Canada and North America in 2011. The label is named after its creative director, hip British designer Alice Temperley, and is renowned for its blend of timeless designs, sumptuous fabrics, and meticulous detail in feminine pieces that embody modern-day "Cool Britannia."

The Accessories With her broad white Stetson and bold belt buckle, the Duchess of Cambridge looked every bit the Canadian cowgirl as she watched the rodeo. William also sported a matching Stetson made of beaver fur with a silk lining. The hats were made by Calgary hatmaker Smithbilt Hats Inc., who have been producing this particular style, which has become an iconic symbol for the city of Calgary,

since the 1940s. They were presented to the royal couple as a gift after they landed at the Calgary International Airport by the mayor, Naheed Nenshi.

Previous members of the Royal Family that have been given the iconic white hat include Prince Philip, Prince Andrew, and Prince Edward. Philip, who received his third hat in 1969, ruffled some feathers when he quipped about not knowing what to do with another hat other than to carry water or plant flowers in it. This prompted the city to give Prince Charles a black cowboy hat when he arrived eight years later.

The Boots While Kate's boots are a traditional cowboy style, like her shirt they are made by a London-based designer. This time she picked the humorously named R. Soles. The label has sold high-quality boots from its store on the King's Road, Chelsea, since being established by Douglas Berney in 1975. Kate's boots are the label's "Vegas Setter" style and were designed by Judy Rothchild.

The Jeans No cowgirl outfit would be complete without a pair of boot-cut jeans, and Kate's come from one of her favorite denim labels: Goldsign. The style is named "Passion," and the Duchess opted for the Habit wash from the label's Fall 2011 collection. Cut narrowly on the hip and slender in the thigh, they are made from Goldsign's famously soft, stretchy denim, making them flatteringly form-fitting and comfortable. In other words, perfect for horseback riding! According to a spokesperson for Goldsign, sales of their jeans tripled after Kate wore this pair, and the company's web traffic increased tenfold.

Kate is not a fan of obvious branding so it's likely that one of the things she loves about Goldsign, a premium denim line started by Adriano Goldschmied, formerly of AG and Diesel, is its tendency toward subtle brand marks with no distinctive labels or back-pockets to look out for. Kate is said to have bought these jeans from Trilogy Stores in Chelsea, London, where she has been a regular customer for the last few years.

Embrace Local Style

Wherever she is in the world, Kate never misses out on the opportunity to have fun and experiment with local fashion—and pay a flattering compliment to her host country at the same time. Here's how she cleverly dresses for the occasion while also bringing her own undeniable personal style to play:

Go for authenticity
Kate's hat is from a reputable Calgary hatmaker, not from a tourist store, and this prevents it from becoming a parody. For true local style, do a little research into an area's designers before you travel.

Keep a sense of identity
Kate cleverly mixes pieces from Calgary with Western-style pieces from London-based designers to create a fusion look that effortlessly brings together her British roots and the Calgary culture.

Understand the importance of timing
Eyebrows were raised when William and Kate didn't immediately don their hats at the airport, but by bringing the hat out at the Calgary Stampede, Kate showed she truly appreciated the value of the gift and that she understood the sense of occasion.

The devil's in the details
Kate put thought into every aspect of her outfit, from the cut of her jeans to the size of her belt buckle. Doing so, rather than just adding tokens of local culture to whatever you're already wearing, will make your outfit work as a considered "look" rather than looking like a costume.

LOOK 9

Kate's Flight of Fancy

The Dress When Kate stepped off the plane at LAX airport on July 8, 2011, she was a breath of fresh air in a dove-gray "Peridot" dress by London-based designer Roksanda Ilincic. The wool-crepe garment is typical of the fluid, draped designs that have made Ilincic a favorite of other high-profile women, including Michelle Obama and Gwyneth Paltrow. With its cap sleeves and pleats that fall from the draped neck to the nipped-in waistband, this piece is ultimately both feminine and flattering.

According to Ilincic, after Kate wore the dress, dozens of customers called her London showroom looking for this piece from her Spring 2011 collection, which had already sold out. Ilincic also heard from several stores who were interested in carrying her line. "This is proof she is a perfect ambassador for British fashion, and fashion in general," Ms. Ilincic said.

The Bag This "Natalie" clutch by L.K. Bennett is one of Kate's all-time favorite bags, something she has been spotted carrying on many an occasion. Its diminutive size and neutral coloring make it the perfect multitasking accessory—a bag that will work seamlessly with almost any outfit—including something as delicate as the dove-gray dress.

The Earrings Kate's "Grace" earrings are from Chelsea designer Kiki McDonough. Simple yet striking, these $1,120 white topaz stud earrings framed with diamonds are understated yet still distinctive, which is exactly how Kate likes her jewelry.

McDonough also made jewels for Diana, Princess of Wales. "I once counted Princess Diana as one of my loyal customers and we always had such fun choosing designs for her to wear," McDonough said. "It's a very special added extra that Catherine now enjoys wearing my designs too. As a 'modern Royal,' Catherine is as chic when dressed down as she is at formal engagements—my jewelry is designed to be worn every day, and Catherine does this beautifully."

BELOW: Since Kate started buying their clutch purses and shoes, British brand L.K. Bennett has become famous around the world for its simple but elegant bags, such as the "Natalie" pictured below. Originally founded in London in 1990 and offering sophisticated shoes and accessories, the store now has outlets around the world and has branched out to produce a range of elegant clothing aimed at meeting the lifestyle needs of modern women like their most famous customer: Catherine, Duchess of Cambridge.

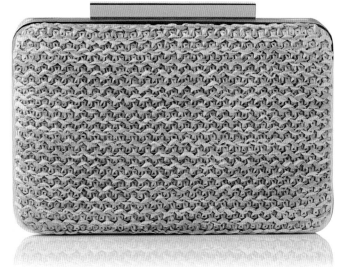

The Shoes Kate's powder-pink "Lovely" stilettos, with a semi-rounded toe and 4.3-inch heel, are from the Jimmy Choo Spring/Summer 2011 collection. They form part of the label's 24:7 capsule collection of bestsellers and classic styles every woman should own.

Kate recently met the label's founder Jimmy Choo during a trip to Malaysia. Choo, who no longer has formal links with the company he created and then sold, worked with Diana, Princess of Wales, for seven years and thought Kate reminiscent of his former friend. "She is an absolutely beautiful person both inside and out," he said of the Duchess. "Very much like Prince's William's mother. They are both elegant and wear fashion well but, most importantly, are very caring people inside, which is why they appear so beautiful in public."

Look Fabulous after a Flight

As part of her royal duties, Kate has racked up plenty of air miles and it is not uncommon for her to have to meet foreign dignitaries straight off a long-haul flight. It is vital that she looks her best on these occasions but clever Kate has gotten fresh-faced fabulousness after a flight down to a fine art.

Change out of flight-worn clothes
Sitting in a plane seat for hours will turn most fabrics into an unattractive bundle of creases. But if you pack like Kate and have a second outfit hanging in your carry-on, ready to change into just before landing, you can ensure your outfit will look flawless as you disembark.

Prepare for temperature changes
Kate boarded the plane bound for chilly Canada in a scarlet satin and wool coatdress by Catherine Walker, perfect for keeping warm, but she knew she'd be emerging under sunny skies in Los Angeles, so she picked out a lighter dress for landing with this in mind.

Moisturize mid-flight
The air on planes is notorious for drying out your skin. For a dewy-fresh glow like Kate's, drink plenty of water and apply moisturizer to your face mid-flight. There's no need to go all out on expensive formulas. Kate has been spotted stocking up on tubs of Nivea Visage Pure & Natural Moisturizing Day Cream at her local pharmacy.

Prepare your hair
Kate boarded the plane with her hair loosely pinned back, ensuring that it would look fresh and bouncy when she unpinned it, just before disembarking at LAX airport.

Feminine Florals

The Dress On July 9, 2011, the royal couple attended a charity polo match at the exclusive Santa Barbara Polo & Racquet Club, which raised money for The American Friends of the Foundation of Prince William and Prince Harry. For the occasion, Kate turned to one of her favorite failsafe designers: Jenny Packham. The Duchess has worn many Packham creations over the past few years, as the designer's romantic, feminine style presents a perfect match for the signature look Kate has carefully crafted. This hand-painted Chinoiserie silk dress in muted blue, sage, and peach tones, featuring cap sleeves and piping, gathers at the shoulder, and cinches at the waist to flatter the Duchess's thin frame.

The exquisite fabric is by artists at Chelsea-based interior design firm de Gournay, which specializes in hand-painted wallpapers, fabrics, and porcelain in eighteenth-century Chinoiserie (the French term for Chinese style) and nineteenth-century French designs. Packham is a big fan of the design house's prints, and her London boutique features the graphical "Windswept Blossom" wallpaper from de Gournay's delightful Eclectic collection.

The Shoes Kate also showcased a new pair of L.K. Bennett shoes—the patent "Sandy" sandal, part of the company's Signature collection. Thick, smooth straps softly wrap around the foot in a very natural way, making the Duchess's legs appear even longer and slimmer.

The Bracelet On her right wrist, Kate wore her gold "C" charm bracelet, a wedding present from her stepmother-in-law, Camilla Parker Bowles, who owns a similar piece. The disc charm has Catherine's official monogram on one side and Camilla's is on the other. Both Cs are under a coronet, but Kate's C has an extra curl, while Camilla's is surrounded by a circle. For Kate, the bracelet clearly holds strong sentimental value, as it is one that she wears often, and she also owns a silver version of it.

The Bag and the Earrings Kate again carried her boxy L.K. Bennett "Natalie" Clutch, and wore Kiki McDonough earrings—this time, an $800 pair of beautiful 18-carat yellow gold citrine drops.

Wear Florals without Looking Frumpy

Bold floral prints can be tricky to pull off, but Kate manages to go floral without looking fussy or frumpy. By sticking to some basic style rules, you can do the same.

Keep accessories simple

All-over florals look stunning when paired with sleek sandals and plain accessories, as Kate has done. The smooth, boxy lines of her bag and shoes make for a calming, elegant contrast to the detailed pattern on her dress—anything too fancy would fight for attention with the print and make the outfit look too busy.

Choose a color

Pick out one feature color from the floral print to echo in your accessories. Kate has chosen the peachy tones of the dress in her neutral shoes and bag, and in doing so has created a look that is cohesive and polished.

Consider the placement of the pattern

Printed fabrics draw the eye, so look closely at which part of the figure is being highlighted by the placement of the print on the body. The positioning of the flowers on Kate's dress works perfectly with its nipped-in waist, creating an hourglass silhouette.

Jenny Packham

A British fashion designer known primarily for her bridal gowns and lingerie-inspired ready-to-wear collections, Jenny Packham has a way of communicating beauty and allure diffused through French lace and beaded tulle. After graduating summa cum laude from Central Saint Martins College of Art and Design in London, she founded Jenny Packham London—designing eveningwear—and launched her first collection at the London Designer Show in 1988. She has been named as Hollywood Style Designer of the Year, International Couture Bridal Designer of the Year 2007, and British Bridal Dress Designer of the Year 2008 and 2011, and her clients include Keira Knightley, Beyoncé, Cameron Diaz, and Jennifer Aniston. The designer's work has been selected for stylistically acclaimed and Oscar-nominated film and television productions, including *Sex and the City*, *The Devil Wears Prada*, *Casino Royale*, and *Die Another Day*.

RIGHT: For her June 10, 2011 outing to the Gala for ARK, the Absolute Return for Kids, the Duchess of Cambridge wore a pearlescent rose sequin gown, embellished with Swarovski crystals, from Jenny Packham's Spring/Summer 2011 collection. Kate paired the dress with L.K. Bennett shoes, staying true to her support of British retailers.

RIGHT: Wearing a silver Grecian-style gown by designer Jenny Packham, draped over one shoulder and gently gathered in at the waist and featuring a bright red poppy, worn for the British veterans' day, Kate dazzled as she and Prince William entertained 120 guests in the Picture Gallery at St. James's Palace on November 10, 2011, at a reception in aid of the National Memorial Arboretum Appeal.

LOOK 11

Kate Does Timeless Glamour

The Dress Even when surrounded by Hollywood's elite, Kate's fashion choices ensure she stands out from the crowd for all the right reasons. Rather than going for a bold color or a daring neckline or hemline, she cleverly stole the spotlight at a July 2011 BAFTA dinner in LA by covering up in a demure, pastel gown. Small touches, such as the shimmering silver belt and full skirt, gave this somewhat conservative outfit the required amount of drama for the high-profile, formal event.

The glamorous Grecian-style pleated dress by Sarah Burton for Alexander McQueen had a soft scoop neck and was pulled tight at the waist by the belt before unfurling a floaty floor-length skirt. Like Kate's wedding dress, the piece appeared to have been custom made for the Duchess by Sarah Burton. This truly was an iconic look for the Princess, and a replica of the gown currently adorns Kate's waxwork at Madame Tussauds in London.

The Bag Kate stuck with her trusty envelope-style clutch purse, but upped the glamour stakes in opting for this dazzling Jimmy Choo "Ubai" clutch in champagne glitter.

The Shoes For her footwear, Kate also went one step beyond her usual nude sandal staples, stepping out in the aptly named "Vamp" sandals by Jimmy Choo. These glittery silver shoes have an open round toe, crossover straps at the front, and a gold buckle-fastening ankle strap. The platform, combined with stiletto heel, makes these dramatic shoes much higher than the classic heels Kate normally wears.

The Jewelry Kate also wore more jewelry than usual for this black-tie gala. On her wrist was a diamond bracelet, boasting a floral cluster design—a large diamond surrounded by smaller diamonds, alternating with baguette diamonds. The bracelet matches the baguette diamonds on her diamond chandelier earrings, which were loaned to her by the Queen especially for the occasion.

Dress Up in Demure Glamour

As a member of the Royal Family, Kate has certain standards to adhere to, so you will never see her in anything vulgar or inappropriate. She always manages to navigate the fine line between looking demure and frumpy. Here's how she pulls off dressing conservatively while still looking incredibly glamorous:

Remember, sexy can be subtle
Rather than choosing a plunging neckline or a short skirt, Kate accentuates her feminine figure by cinching in the flowing fabric of the dress at the waist to create a silhouette with curves in all the right places.

Take it up a level
For the BAFTA dinner, the Duchess wore shoes with higher heels than she normally wears. Stepping out of your comfort zone on special occasions will ensure you look like you've made an effort and haven't just showed up in your everyday clothes.

Color is key
While bold brights will get you instantly noticed, soft but unexpected shades, such as the lilac of Kate's gown, are far more scene-stealing in a subtle way, as they give you a glowing, ethereal air, which is ultimately more memorable.

Bring on the bling
Kate's sparkling shoes and clutch would have looked over-the-top with an equally glittery gown, but if your dress is demure, it allows you to go to town with your accessories.

Whiter Shades of Pale

The Dress Kate shows off a slender and perfectly tailored figure in this oatmeal Amanda Wakeley dress on her visit to the Royal Marsden hospital to meet young cancer sufferers in September 2011. For the royal couple, this was a trip imbued with special meaning, as three decades earlier, Diana, Princess of Wales, had toured the hospital in Sutton, Surrey, on her first solo engagement in 1982. Diana later became the cancer hospital's president—a position that Prince William has filled since 2007.

Princess Diana was famously a big fan of Wakeley's creations, which made the British designer a very appropriate choice for Kate and a stylish way to give a respectful nod to the mother-in-law she never had the chance to meet. Kate's knee-length felt dress featured three-quarter length sleeves, seam details, and a slash neckline, and was purchased from the Amanda Wakeley store in London. The designer later tweeted that the Duchess also bought the same dress in both black and gunmetal—something trendsetters often do when they find a shape that is perfect for them, and a sign that by this point Kate had become very confident of exactly what works as part of her signature "look."

The Shoes Here we see Kate return to her all-time favorite shoes—those taupe "Sledge" heels by L.K. Bennett. The dedicated Duchess has worn these heels for an exhausting list of occasions, including the Epsom Derby, Prince Philip's 90th birthday, Zara Phillips's wedding, on the royal barge during the Queen's Jubilee celebrations, no less than six times during her tour of Canada in 2011, and to numerous engagements on the tour of Asia in 2012. Her repeated wearing of these heels soon had the "Kate Effect" and single-handedly started the popular trend for wearing nude-colored shoes with dresses. In fact, for much of 2011 and 2012, no self-respecting woman would be seen sporting any other footwear.

Kate's devotion to this particular style and shade has caused fashion critics to speculate on whether she owns a dozen pairs exactly the same, because they never look the slightest bit worn! We should perhaps give L.K. Bennett the credit, and view this as testament to how well made the shoes are; given the number of times Kate has worn them, they must be both comfortable and durable, despite their 4-inch heel. Her "Natalie" gold clutch with its woven straw exterior is another L.K. Bennett design that is a staple for Kate.

The Jewelry On this occasion, the Duchess of Cambridge posed a conundrum for the eagle-eyed press: the curious case of the missing jewels. She arrived at the hospital wearing

Working Winter White

Kate has said that her favorite color is white, and she certainly picks a great number of white or off-white shades throughout the seasons. Examples of her preferred hue include the ruffled Reiss dress worn for her official engagement photographs, her Alexander McQueen sailor dress, and a selection of Temperley blouses worn on the 2011 royal tour. Here's how she makes this tricky shade work to her advantage—even in the coldest months:

Get the shade right
Outside of June to August, Kate knows it's best to steer away from bright true whites and choose slightly warmer off-white shades such as ivory, cream, or champagne, as they look less summery and more elegant.

Don't be afraid to flash a little flesh
If the weather is warm enough—as it was on this glorious late September day—and, like Kate, you still have a summer tan, there's nothing wrong with revealing your legs. But, by wearing longer sleeves, she cleverly ensures the dress is still season-appropriate.

Fabric is key
Forget the cottons and linens of summer— as the weather cools, winter whites should be worn in heavier fabrics with more texture. For the hospital visit, Kate chose a dress of seamed felt, but fine-knit wools such as cashmere, light tweeds, or mid-weight jersey would have worked equally well.

Nude rules
For a long time, Kate has known that flesh-toned shoe shades blend into the background with any outfit, while simultaneously making legs look slimmer, longer, and shapelier. This makes them the perfect accompaniment to fall or winter white outfits, rather than white shoes, which can look tacky, or black, which may appear too harsh with a pale ensemble.

her sapphire and diamond engagement ring, but it seemed to have vanished by the time she left, two hours later. Of course, there was a simple explanation. Rather than misplacing it, the Duchess simply stowed it in her clutch purse for hygiene reasons, on the advice of hospital staff.

Along with her ring, Kate also wore her much-loved, diamond-studded silver cross pendant and diamond "Grace" earrings, both by designer Kiki McDonough.

Amanda Wakeley

A self-taught designer, born in Chester, England, who worked for Go Silk in New York before launching her own label in 1990, Amanda Wakeley has developed an international reputation for designing stylish, supremely luxurious, womenswear and accessories. Primarily known for her timeless, luxury eveningwear and pared-down classic daywear, which she describes as "simple ideas expressed strongly," she also has successful shoe and fine jewelry collections. Her ready-to-wear and bespoke creations are sold in the U.K., U.S.A., Europe, and the Middle East, and she has dressed such stars as Scarlett Johansson, Demi Moore, Kate Beckinsale, Charlize Theron, Jada Pinkett Smith, Helen Mirren, and Kate Winslet, and created many of the dresses in the 2012 Bond film, *Skyfall*. She has also dressed many members of royal families, including the late Princess of Wales, whom she provided with many of her most feminine suits, including the bottle-green executive suit Princess Diana wore when she resigned from public life in 1993.

OPPOSITE: Kate wore this floor-length, aqua-colored Amanda Wakeley evening gown, with flowing Grecian-style pleated chiffon, to her first official solo engagement at the In Kind Direct charity reception in October 2011.

RIGHT: Kate chose Wakeley again here, donning this charcoal knee-length frock, accessorized with an Alexander McQueen belt, for a reception at the Imperial War Museum Foundation in April 2012.

It's a Wrap

The Dress When Kate and William visited Centrepoint's Camberwell Foyer in London on a chilly December 21, 2011, the Duchess once again perfectly judged the mood of the occasion when picking out her outfit. The dressed-down elegance of Kate's olive green sweater dress was just what was called for when it came to an event that included a healthy cooking session with some of the homeless young people that the Centrepoint charity supports. The dress is by Ralph Lauren Blue Label, the American brand's most mainstream collection, making it once again that perfect midpoint of aspirational and accessible. Kate may have been covered up in long sleeves and a turtleneck, but the form-fitting nature of her lambswool and cashmere dress ensured she oozed classic winter glamour.

The Belt Kate's tight-fitting, wide-gauge belt draws the eye to her size 2 waist and, if reports are to be believed, this was exactly the effect that the Duchess wanted to create. After the event, seasoned fashion followers believe Kate wore this figure-hugging outfit to put an end to the endless pregnancy speculation she faced in the months following the Royal Wedding.

The Boots Kate paired her sweater dress with opaque pantyhose and her trusty "Hi and Dry" boots from Aquatalia by Marvin K. She has worked these on many occasions, unsurprising when you consider the classic calf-high boots are not only stylish and flattering but eminently practical. Advertised as no-slip boots, the resistant rubber soles are topped with weatherproof stretch suede, making them a must-have staple for someone who often has to step out in the erratic British weather. The durability is down to Aquatalia's Canadian founder Marvin Krasnow, known simply as "Marvin K." Witnessing the harsh effects of Montreal winters on women's footwear, Krasnow set out to provide the luxury of looking good while standing up to the elements. Little wonder British fan Kate frequently purchases his creations at U.K. retailer Russell & Bromley, where they are sold exclusively.

ABOVE: When Kate visited Newcastle's Civic Centre in October 2012, she demonstrated her skill for using a stylish wide belt to dress up a simple outfit and create a more figure-flattering shape. This black leather belt with its large gold buckle is the perfect finishing touch to the plum wool coat she wears here.

Glam Up a Sweater Dress

Wool may not be the obvious choice for a sleek outfit, but Kate has mastered the art of transforming a cozy wardrobe basic—the sweater dress—into a classic seasonal staple. By following her lead, you can look effortlessly chic, even when wrapped up warm for winter.

Balance is key
Kate chooses pantyhose, as bare legs would look unbalanced when paired with black boots, long sleeves, and a turtleneck. In opting for a pair of opaques, she ensures her outfit looks composed.

Avoid excess bulk
Wearing wool from neck to knee could add unflattering inches, but opting for a clingy, fine knit creates a flattering silhouette.

Best foot forward
To instantly transform a sweater dress from daywear to eveningwear, slip on some sleek high heels.

Belt up
If, like Kate, you want to show off your small frame, draw attention to your waist with a broad-waisted belt. If, however, you're a little less body-confident, you can fake an hourglass shape by wearing your belt slightly lower, across the top of your hips, to create a smooth line and cover up any lumps and bumps.

Wear studs with high necks
Kate keeps it simple with Kiki McDonough's white topaz and diamond earrings (see opposite).

Kate Gets Her Game On

The Jacket Not one to be left at home by the fire, Kate bundled up in this luxurious chocolate-colored sheepskin jacket and braved the elements to watch Princes William and Harry play a Christmas Eve soccer match in 2011. Part of the L.K. Bennett Signature collection, the "Darwin" coat is a truly timeless piece that we're sure the Duchess will be sheltering behind for many winters to come. With its narrow waist and full collar and cuffs, and exposed sheepskin, this is the ultimate in classic feminine winter tailoring.

The Sweater Underneath her jacket, Kate layered on warmth with a cozy cream turtleneck "Honeycomb Tunic" sweater by Alice Temperley. The lambswool classic is said to be one of Temperley's first designs, and the honeycomb detail on its collar and sleeves has proved to be so popular that it has become a trademark of Temperley's key collections, with the pattern now being featured on everything from capes to dresses.
Winter fashion is all about luxurious fabrics in textures irresistible to the touch, and you can't get much more tactile than Kate's lambswool sweater and sheepskin jacket combo. The sweater's slouchy cream collar frames the face perfectly, complementing her glowing complexion.

The Jeans Kate's jeans are the "Straight" jeans by Twenty8Twelve, the label founded by sisters Sienna and Savannah Miller. Both have slender figures similar to the Duchess, which may explain why their designs work so well on her. These dark blue, straight-leg jeans are made from flattering stretch denim, making them ideal for casual day-in-the-park chic.

The Boots Not one to put a wrong foot in the fashion stakes, Kate slipped on a pair of green "Vierzon" wellington boots by Le Chameau for the game. A French brand, Le Chameau were founded in 1927 in rainy Normandy, and have specialized in upscale country attire ever since. Their boots are handmade from natural rubber with a luxurious leather lining to keep feet dry and warm on the dampest of days. Kate relies on her trusty Vierzons for any occasion involving outdoor pursuits, and the "Duchess Effect" has not gone unnoticed by the brand.

"Having the Princess regularly pictured in Le Chameau is great news for us," confirms Karl Waktare, managing director of LLC Ltd, which imports Le Chameau products into the U.K. "We are the brand of choice for true country people, like Kate."

The Hat Kate completes her look with a brown Australian safari-style hat, which she has owned for many years and often wears on country strolls to protect her trademark glossy mane from the elements.

Look like a Good Sport

Kate has been attending William's sporting events since they began dating, back at St. Andrews University. Not one to dress up in a tacky fan's shirt, over the years she has developed her own brand of classic supporter chic. Now you can do the same.

Practical can be pretty
Leave the high heels and dresses to the reality shows! Boots or sneakers and pants are far more appropriate for cheering from the sidelines and have their own stylish country feel.

Bundle up
There is nothing less attractive than being covered in goose bumps, shivering on the sidelines. Opt for chunky, warm layers that will give you the stamina to stay till the end of the game, no matter how chilly it is.

Comfort is key
Kate's soft fabrics and denim are no coincidence. When you know that you are going to stand around for a while, the right choice of fabric makes all the difference between looking at ease or being uncomfortable.

Keep shapes feminine
Kate's jacket narrows at the waist, meaning that, despite the warm layers, she still shows off her fabulous figure.

LOOK 15

Buttoned-up Beauty

The Coat While many of us may be guilty of overlooking the importance of the right coat for an outdoor engagement, Kate puts a lot of thought into her outer layer. For the unveiling of a plaque by HM the Queen at luxury foodstore Fortnum & Mason, to commemorate the regeneration of the Piccadilly area of London, Kate chose a single-breasted, collarless coat. The twin daffodils on the lapel are to celebrate the date: March 1, St. David's Day, 2012.

Selected from the Fall/Winter 2010 collection of M by Missoni, the Italian brand's more affordable diffusion line, the coat has an interesting fringe trim made from blue bouclé —a type of yarn that produces a knotted, rough-textured fabric. Italian fashion house Missoni is famous for its colorful knitwear. The family-run brand was launched in 1953 when Tai and Rosita Missoni began producing their signature crochet-knit designs in Varese. Now, headed by daughter Angela, Missoni continues to deliver exquisite collections with inimitable Italian flair.

Kate's choice of coat proved once again that she has a real eye for a style bargain—not only is the coat from Missoni's more affordable line, the Duchess actually picked it up for a discount price in an outlet store. An assistant at the Missoni store at the Bicester Village outlet in Oxfordshire confirmed that Kate bought the dress there. "We were all surprised to see her and it was great to see her wearing it alongside the Queen."

The Shoes Kate's sense of sartorial fun came into play with her choice of ladylike gray suede pumps by Rupert Sanderson. Like every pair of Sanderson shoes, these "Malone" pumps are named after a daffodil, making them a fitting way for Kate to mark St. David's Day and highlighting her incredible eye for detail.

Rather than troubling with elaborate embellishment, Rupert Sanderson's design ethos is "less is more"—his focus is on perfecting the line, balance, and symmetry of the shoe to flatter and lengthen the leg. With their rounded toe and slender heels, these understated pumps are a chic and timeless choice, typical of Kate.

The Earrings Kate's ears were adorned with her white topaz and white rhodolite "Hope Egg" earrings by Links of London, previously worn during the official engagement photograph, shot by Mario Testino. Hope eggs are an important symbol in Russian culture, representing hope and new life. Once more the "Kate Effect" was felt in full force after the Duchess first wore these simple earrings, with a fight reportedly breaking out in one New York Links of London store over the last pair!

Snag a Designer Bargain

Kate's known as the "thrifty Royal" for good reason. The Duchess has a real eye for a bargain and is savvy enough to know where to find them.

Hit the outlets
Kate bought her M by Missoni coat at discount center Bicester Village, which consists of 130 outlet boutiques, including highly sought-after designer brands such as Céline, Dior, Alexander McQueen, Prada, and Mulberry, all selling past season and end-of-line pieces with discounts of up to 60 percent. Queen of the Sales Kate said she loved the discount shopping destination in Oxfordshire as "everything is so contained."

Search for second-hand
Kate is also said to often pick up designer pieces from a secondhand store called The Stock Exchange, near her parents' home in the Berkshire village of Bucklebury. It stocks nearly-new designer clothes by Miu Miu, Issa, and Gucci, and is very popular with the locals.

Get in the know
Kate's lucky enough to be courted by fashion industry insiders so she'll always know when there's a sample sale going on. But you can also get in on the insider knowledge by signing up to your favorite labels and boutique mailing lists to receive "early bird" notice of any upcoming secret sales.

Olympic Fashion Feats

The Blazer Selecting a comfortable ensemble for a relaxed visit to the Team GB hockey squad at the London 2012 Olympic Park on March 15, 2012, Kate reworked the classic "Sloane" blazer and jeans look of her youth. The Duchess of Cambridge, here acting as an Olympic Ambassador, mixed high fashion with retail pieces to create her own take on business casual. Her double-breasted "Punto Milano" jacket is by Italian design house Pucci.

Beloved by style icons such as Jackie O, brand founder Emilio Pucci's kaleidoscopic prints were an instant hit during the 1950s. Now under the directorship of Norwegian designer Peter Dundas, the iconic label's bold clothing continues to impress. This particular blazer, however, is a pretty classic piece of tailoring, with its bright gold buttons and shoulder pads, but the exacting cut elevates Kate's look from the everyday to sharp styling.

The Scarf In place of her usual glittering necklace, Kate wore an official Team GB supporter's scarf. The red, white, and blue scarf was sold at Next.com, and all profits made from its sale were channeled back into the British Olympic and British Paralympic Associations. As an official Ambassador for Team GB, Kate was expected to wear the scarf several times during the Games. Note how she echoes the scarf's Union Jack color scheme in her navy jacket, white tee, and coral jeans—a clever show of solidarity with the British athletes she was meeting.

The Jeans Kate caused a stir when she stepped out in these coral jeans, and not just because of their vibrant color. Fashion watchers' tongues were set wagging as it wasn't clear if the pair came from one of her favorite denim designers, J Brand, or if they were a budget choice of "Pop Slim Fit" jeans from Kate's chain store staple, Zara. Around the same time, the Duchess was also spied performing her Olympic duties in a pair of bright cobalt-blue jeans and a vivid red blazer, both from Zara, lending weight to the theory that she was buying her denim from chain stores.

The effect of Kate wearing this trendy shade was immediate. Just 24 hours later, George at Asda witnessed an 88 percent surge in sales of their lookalike pair, soon to be dubbed "tan-ger-jeans." Fiona Lambert, brand director at George at Asda, said: "Wearing bright colors lifts us all, and now we have the royal seal of approval for colored denim from Kate Middleton, we know this is going to be the hot trend this summer. Kate looks fabulous in her coral skinny jeans, so girls all over the country will be emulating her style and we expect sales to continue to go through the roof."

Aside from anticipating the colored denim trend, Kate also worked another key look of the season, as she rolled up the jeans' legs to make them three-quarter length. It is exactly these little personalized touches that help make Kate a serious trendsetter.

Find Your Perfect Blazer

Blazers are such a wardrobe staple that every woman should own at least one. They can be dressed up or down, as Kate showed when she wore the same Emilio Pucci blazer with a pencil skirt when presenting medals at the Paralympics later in the month. With a little royal fashion know-how, anyone can turn a classic blazer into an item that will carry them through any occasion.

The perfect fit
One reason why Kate always looks so chic in a blazer is because she goes for styles that fit like a glove. To ensure yours fits properly, do the arm-lift test—you should be able to raise your arms without the jacket restricting your movement, even when fully buttoned. In addition, the shoulder seam should sit squarely on the shoulders. If the seam is off your shoulders, the jacket is too large and will make you look sloppy.

Single or double?
Double-breasted jackets such as Kate's look great on slimmer figures, but if you're curvy, the additional row of buttons can make you appear top-heavy, so stick to single-breasted shapes.

Color coordinate
To get the most wear out of your blazer, select one in a neutral color such as black or navy, which will then work with every color of the rainbow. This gives you the option of wearing the same blazer for different occasions, yet making it look fresh every single time. Because Kate's jacket is in classic navy, she can experiment with bright jeans or dress it up with a printed skirt.

Keeping Style in the Family

The Dress Kate made her first public speech as a member of the Royal Family at The Treehouse children's hospice in Ipswich, Suffolk, on March 19, 2012. In order to gain confidence for the event, she slipped into something familiar. The bright blue "Trina" dress from Kate's chain-store favorite Reiss was first worn by Carole Middleton, Kate's mother, at Ascot in 2010. Kate has, in fact, styled it in almost exactly the same way—wearing the thick black belt that came with the dress and a pair of simple black heels. Reassuring it may have been, but the outfit did attract one or two negative comments from members of the press who felt that it was just a tad too large for Kate and hung loosely off her slender frame.

But while the double-breasted coatdress was arguably a little busy, with an oversized collar and scoop pockets designed to draw the eye, Kate still pulls off the look by keeping her accessories simple to create a clean overall outline.

It was also good to see the Duchess sticking to one of her standby British brands, which meant she was helping to boost the U.K. economy at the same time as giving us all a lesson in family recycling. Her speech, it should be noted, was described as "faultless."

The Fundraising Bracelet Kate's left wrist was adorned with a brightly colored beaded fundraising bracelet from EACH—East Anglia's Children's Hospices. She is a Royal Patron for the charity that support families and cares for children with life-threatening conditions. Interestingly, the bracelet was designed for EACH by Imogen Sheeran, whose son is the well-known British popstar Ed Sheeran.

The Diamond Bracelet On her right wrist, Kate wore her Tiffany "Diamonds by the Yard" bracelet—a sterling-silver piece adorned with round brilliant diamonds to catch the light, which was created for Tiffany by Elsa Peretti. The Italian jewelry designer is famous for creating understated and timeless pieces, and also designed the necklace Kate wore when the royal engagement was announced.

The Shoes Kate's patent pumps are the "Angel" style by the label Episode, which is known for its elegant accessories and well-cut clothing and is exclusive to British department store House of Fraser. They have a small platform under the toe, which make them a perfectly practical choice when the Duchess needs comfort in order to concentrate on the task at hand.

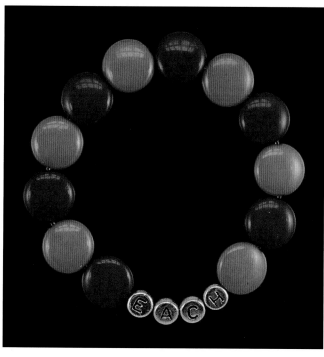

LEFT: Normally a fan of more demure jewelry, Kate raised a few eyebrows when she wore this candy-inspired bracelet, but it was quickly learned that it was in support of a charity close to her heart. The bright purple and orange beads, which featured four round metallic stones that read EACH, was specially commissioned for the East Anglia Children's Hospice. The bracelet's designer, Imogen Sheeran, is mother to English singer-songwriter Ed Sheeran, and much of Sheeran's jewelry, including this piece, is said to be inspired by Ed's favorite candies.

NEXT SPREAD: Kate shows off her bold color-blocking sartorial skills with these two strikingly elegant ensembles. The flowing red silk jersey "Sarai" evening gown, left, with billowing sleeves, plunging V-neck, and sash waist, is by Beulah London, worn when she and Prince WIlliam attended a gala for the Child Bereavement Charity in October 2011. The canary-yellow Jaegar shirt dress, right, was worn for her visit to the Solomon Islands in September 2012, and features a full, pleated skirt and tie-waist.

Wow in Primary Colors

Primary colors make a big impact and draw a lot of attention. You have to be confident in your fashion choice to wear a bold color as Kate often does on formal occasions, like the 2012 Jubilee engagements. In making brave fashion choices, she was honoring the importance of key events during a special year for the Royal Family. Here's how you can create the right impact with color:

Red—Bear the season in mind
There is an important distinction to be made between rich festive red and hot summer red. Brighter shades such as the scarlet Alexander McQueen dress worn by Kate aboard the royal barge during the Thames Diamond Jubilee Pageant evoke the freshness of summer without any of the heaviness of deeper winter tones, such as berry.

Yellow—Dare to turn heads
A bright yellow dress is definitely a defiant fashion choice—it's a shade that simply demands attention. Avoid diluting this affect by wearing yellow with other colors, though. Be brave and make yellow the solo hero of your outfit, just as Kate did when she paired her yellow Jaeger shirt dress with nude heels when visiting the Solomon Islands on her royal tour in September 2012.

Blue—Be bright
Blue is often seen as a neutral color, especially in darker shades like navy. But blue can make just as much of a statement as other primaries if you opt for bright shades, such as Kate's electric-blue Reiss dress, seen on page 78.

Kate's Animal Attraction

The Dress April 25, 2012, was a fashion first for Kate when she wore celebrated British designer Matthew Williamson on a visit to the British Film Institute for the London première of *African Cats*. The royal couple were there to see the Disney documentary, which had been made in conjunction with the Tusk Trust—a charity Prince William has been a Royal Patron of since 2005. The movie tells the story of a family of cheetahs and a pride of lions, and aims to raise awareness and funds for the animal protection charity.

Kate had never previously worn anything by designer-to-the-stars Williamson for an official occasion, but his beautifully cut gowns featuring vivacious embroidery and eye-catching detailing fit perfectly into the Duchess's existing fashion repertoire. This sleek gray dress is from Williamson's Pre-Fall 2012 collection and features ornate beading, an exposed zipper in the back, and the subtle peplum detailing that Kate became so fond of in 2012.

The dress has three-quarter length sleeves and deep turquoise and gold beads around the neck and sleeves. Williamson added more beading at the neck especially for Kate's frock, which was not present on the catwalk version. These signature Williamson flourishes cleverly harmonized with the movie's African vibe.

Matthew Williamson's label is now 15 years old, during which time the graduate of the famous Central Saint Martins College of Art and Design in London has become renowned for celebrity-beloved butterfly-print dresses and his line of bridal gowns and accessories. In 2011, the designer also launched a more moderately priced collection—MW Matthew Williamson—and has had a lower-end collection—Butterfly by Matthew Williamson—available at U.K. retailer Debenhams since 2009. These easily affordable lines have brought a taste of his luxurious and feel-good designs to the masses without compromising the integrity of his core approach—no tough feat for such a high-profile designer!

The Earrings Once more, Kate turned to her favorite jewelry designer, Kiki McDonough, for her stunning blue topaz and diamond pear earrings that perfectly dovetail with the detailing on her dress. The eye-catching "Kiki Classic" earrings soon became runaway bestsellers, despite their rather hefty price tag of $2,000.

The Shoes and Bag Kate let her dress do all the talking by pairing it with these understated carbon-gray suede "Valerie" pumps and matching clutch purse, both from British shoe designer Emmy Scarterfield, a favorite of the Duchess. She also has the same shoe and bag combination in brown. Scarterfield is the founder of the luxury custom-made wedding and dress shoe brand Emmy Shoes. Having worked in Milan, designing shoes for five years, she set up the brand after struggling to find comfortable but pretty occasion shoes.

Perfect Occasion Makeup

Kate always manages to fit her cosmetic choices to perfectly suit the occasion, and with her consistently flawless skin, glowing cheeks, and expertly defined eyes, it's hard to believe that most of the time she insists on doing her own makeup! Here are some of her easy-to-follow tricks:

Look after your skin
You only have to look as far as mom, Carole, to see that Kate owes her amazing complexion in part to good genes. But the Duchess is also said to stick to a consistent cleanse, tone, and moisturize skincare routine, wherever she is in the world. This means she usually only needs a touch of light foundation or tinted moisturizer as a base.

Keep colors neutral
Kate is never one to shy away from color, but she saves it all for her vibrant wardrobe, which is full of rich jewel tones. When it comes to makeup, her cheeks tend to have a subtle rosy-pink flush, while on her lips she usually goes for a gloss just a shade or two darker than her natural lip color.

Pick one feature to emphasize
The beauty rule goes: eyes or lips, but never both. Kate follows this rule religiously and pretty much always opts for eyes. She rims both her upper and lower lash lines with black eyeliner and a generous layer of mascara. This creates a look that is always striking, but never overdone.

Pale but perfect nails
When you have a stunning wedding band and eye-catching sapphire engagement ring to show off, you don't want to upstage them with brightly colored nail polish. Kate's nails are always neatly trimmed and filed, and tend to be covered with a simple baby-pink varnish.

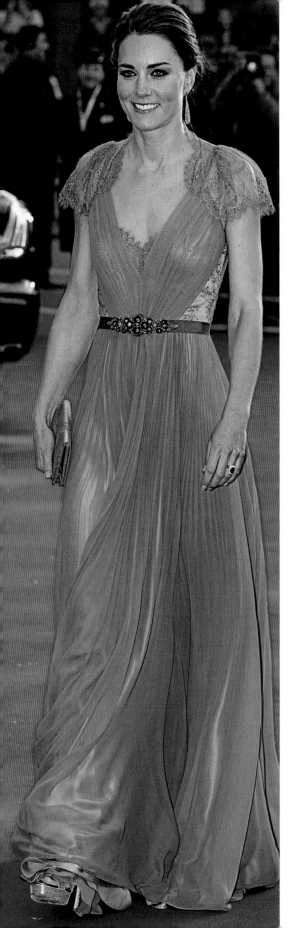

The Striking Appeal of Teal

The Dress On May 11, 2012, Kate and Prince William were guests of honor at the Greatest Team Rises Olympic gala event—an official launch party for Team GB and ParalympicsGB, which helped mark the final countdown to the London 2012 Games. For such a high-energy occasion, Kate wowed in one of her bravest fashion choices to date: this stunning Jenny Packham teal ballgown, marking a welcome return to one of her favorite designers. She chose a custom version of Packham's "Aspen" gown, which first appeared on the catwalk in a pale green shade as part of her Spring/Summer 2012 collection.

The neckline was also more demure than the catwalk gown, with extra gathered fabric in the bodice and slightly higher lace at the décolletage and shoulders. But Kate's head-turning teal shade drew maximum attention to a design that boasts beautiful silk chiffon, lacy cap sleeves, an ornately embellished bodice, bejewelled waistband, and flowing pleated skirt. Perhaps the most show-stopping feature was the gown's button-up back, made entirely from lace and dotted with sparkling Swarovski crystals—beautifully delicate, but also subtly sexy.

Of course, this was far from the first time Kate had turned to Jenny Packham to pack a red carpet punch. The Duchess has worn the British's designer's regal creations on many previous occasions, including the silver one-shoulder gown accented by a velvet ribbon that she wore as host of a charity dinner at St. James's Palace in November 2011, and the dazzling pearlescent rose sequin gown, again decorated with Swarovski crystals, worn at the ARK children's charity gala dinner in June 2011, which was the first event Kate and Prince William attended as a married couple.

The Hair This is one dress that demanded an "up-do" rather than Kate's beloved loose-flowing blow-dried waves, and the Duchess elected for an elaborate style featuring multiple braided sections forming an intricate chignon. An elegant knotted bun, put in place by the team from the Richard Ward salon in Chelsea, London, that Kate—and her family—have long frequented, showed off the elaborate bodice design on the reverse of her dress to full effect. The swept-to-one-side part—a new look for Kate—also gave the style added height and impact from the front.

The Shoes and Bag Kate accessorized the striking dress with a matching custom clutch purse, again by Jenny Packham, made from the same silk as the gown and a layer of the brocade used in its side panels. The look was completed by a pair of high-octane glamour Jimmy Choo platform "Vamp" sandals, in distressed silver leather, which she has worn on other occasions.

The Finishing Touches The Duchess completed her glamorous look with silver teardrop-shaped diamanté earrings. Her makeup, meanwhile, featured the new addition of some shimmery eyeshadow to complement her signature smoky black mascara and eyeliner, plus a shiny pale pink gloss for her lips.

Channel 1950s Glamour like Kate

For show-stopping events, Kate often favors a classic 1950s-style lace and silk formal gown. This was first seen in her vintage choice of wedding dress by Sarah Burton for Alexander McQueen, but you can also note the 1950s flavors in this teal Jenny Packham number. It's a look that openly references former Hollywood movie icons and was most typified by the effortless chic of another regal style icon: movie star and Princess of Monaco, Grace Kelly. So it's no surprise that similarities were drawn between Kate's choice of wedding gown and the lace-bodiced number worn by Kelly for her marriage to Prince Rainier in 1956. Here's how to borrow some of this retro look:

Draw attention to your waist
Tiny waists are top priority for any fifties' bombshell, and Kate draws attention to her hourglass figure by choosing frocks that gather in tightly at the waist.

Find a fitted bodice
For this look, above-the-waist dresses should be tight fitting and, ideally, have a sweetheart neckline. Gowns tend to be strapless and bare-shouldered, although a thin veil of see-through lace or chiffon is often stretched over the décolletage and arm area for a demure finish.

Full-length flow
Although full, prom-style skirts were very popular in the 1950s, not all evening gown designs were dominated by this look. Long, sleek lines were also in vogue, as echoed here in Kate's Jenny Packham frock, and styles were sometimes reminiscent of wedding gowns or nightgowns. To emulate this look, the fabric should be silk or satin, the dress floor-length, fitted at the waist and oozing a mixture of class and old-fashioned sex appeal.

Don't forget to sparkle
Finishing touches are critical for true movie-style glamour, with Kate and Grace Kelly both favoring diamond or diamanté embellishments sewn into gowns and onto clutch purses, and showcasing the same precious stones when it comes to earrings and necklaces. This ensures the maximum light is reflected when those inevitable flashes go off!

LOOK 20

Polo with Polish

The Dress When you're a spectator, it's never a good idea to draw attention away from the main event. So when Kate went to watch Princes William and Harry play polo at the Audi Polo Challenge at Coworth Park in Berkshire, England, in May 2012, she chose a pretty, yet subtle green dress.

This is the "Rebecca" dress—from another label Kate loves to wear: Hampshire-based British designer Libélula. This knee-length dress, from the label's Fall/Winter 2011 collection, is 100 percent silk and features side pockets, plus piping at the collar, cuffs, and waist.

Kate chose the buttoned-up printed shift in the popular "mermaid blue and brown petal" version, but the dress also came in a brighter "emerald green with cream petals," a plain green (see right, center), and a black-and-white polka dot, as well as a more formal version in black velvet.

It is perhaps no coincidence that the Libélula line is designed by Sophie Cranston, who early in her career, worked with two other labels adored by Kate: Alexander McQueen and Temperley. In fact, the Duchess is such a firm fan of Libélula that, before the Royal Wedding, Cranston was almost Kate's dress designer of choice, although Sarah Burton for Alexander McQueen famously won the final commission.

Nevertheless, Cranston's vibrant prints and timeless shapes, crafted from luxurious fabrics, have proved popular with a number of celebrities, including Emma Watson and Jerry Hall. One of the more notable Libélula items that Kate has also worn is the "Dulwich" coat—a black velvet number that sold out hours after she was snapped wearing it to a friend's wedding in January 2011.

The Shoes Kate donned a pair of camel Stuart Weitzman "Minx" espadrilles to match her green dress—towering wedges that made her legs look even longer and more defined than usual. Each shoe base is crafted from cork and boasts a huge 4.5-inch heel, so they're not for the faint-hearted. However, despite their vertiginous shape, the espadrilles actually demonstrate Kate's practical side. After watching William play polo for more than 10 years now, she is well aware that wedges are actually a perfect choice since they won't sink into the grass. The wedges are especially useful during the popular ritual when spectators are called upon to "tread in the divots" between chukkas. This amusing but crucial part of polo involves stamping in loose pieces of turf that the horses have kicked up during the game, helping to ensure the grass is as flat as possible before play is resumed.

Country Chic with a Modern Twist

Whether she's neat and classic in a simple dress or more dressed-down in jeans and boots, Kate knows exactly how to work country style like a true native. It's a look that has its roots in jodhpurs and riding boots, and floral Laura Ashley-style dresses, but this uniform has been updated by the Duchess to include skinny jeans, long leather boots, and more stylish designer pieces. This cleverly ensures she fits in seamlessly with the country crowd that she has married into, while maintaining her own signature style. Here are some of the key fashion rules for fitting right in:

Try some tweed

It doesn't have to be stuffy or boring—in fact, this once old-fashioned fabric has recently made a comeback. Kate knows that, when used in moderation, tweed can look fabulous in the form of a fitted jacket or simple accessory, such as a tote bag.

Wear shoes you can walk in

Kate appreciates that no outdoor event is much fun unless you can move around comfortably all day. The ability to move quickly is especially vital as she so often brings the young couple's much-loved dog, Lupo, with her for this kind of event. Here, she's wearing wedges, but she is just as frequently seen in long, flat-heeled, leather riding-style boots.

Be prepared

With all the rain in the U.K., good rain boots are a countryside necessity. Rain boots now come in a rainbow of colors and prints, with designers such as Marc Jacobs and Patrick Cox making their own limited edition pairs featuring edgier details such as bejewelled buckles, high heels, and mock-croc textures. Kate used to be seen in popular high-end Hunters, but in 2012 switched to a pair of green "Vierzon" boots by French brand Le Chameau.

Libélula

Designed by Sophie Cranston, Libélula is an innovative up-and-coming British design house based in Hampshire, England.

After starting her career in fashion in the backrooms of Savile Row and Bellville Sassoon, Cranston went on to work for Alexander McQueen, and then set up Temperley in 2000 with Alice Temperley. After a move to the south of Spain, Cranston founded Libélula, meaning "dragonfly" in Spanish. A return to the U.K. saw the brand expand into many of the leading boutiques and also internationally.

Known for its vibrant prints and timeless and flattering shapes, as well as Cranston's innate sense of color and use of luxurious fabrics, the label creates classics with a twist, like the elegant, black velvet "Dulwich" coat with a diamanté clasp, seen here. Libélula also has a range of wedding dresses and bridesmaids dresses in their signature shapes and fabrics.

The "Kate Effect" has definitely benefited the company. "Kate has helped the business enormously," Cranston told British *Vogue*. "She has had an amazing effect on the label." In describing the inspirations that drive the label, the designer says, "I have tried to make dresses that can be worn every day with some eveningwear … I have mixed fabrics: such as velvet with lace, and wool with lace, as well as different silks mixed together."

LOOK 21

Pretty in Pink

The Dress Kate chose to wear this dusky pink formal Emilia Wickstead coatdress for the World Sovereign's lunch to celebrate the Queen's Diamond Jubilee at Windsor Castle on May 18, 2012. The dress needed to feel suitably regal, as the event was attended by an impressive who's who of modern royalty, with over 60 attendees from around the globe, including an impressive 24 kings and queens!

Made from double-wool crepe, the soft pink frock with a full pleated skirt featured a fitted bodice, with concealed off-center closure and an inset waistband. The minimalist approach, with long sleeves and modest hemline, made for a fittingly demure effect, considering the esteemed company.

Kate's dress came from Emilia Wickstead's Spring/ Summer 2012 collection, which featured a pretty array of candy-box colors, and was described by the designer as being a "mixture of sophistication and playfulness—for fashionable women who entertain."

The Duchess of Cambridge has been one of Wickstead's most famous fans, opting for her garments on numerous public engagements when the eyes of the world have been upon her, and Kate has also been spotted several times visiting the designer's atelier in London's Belgravia.

Kate particularly loves Wickstead's signature classy-but-simple dresses and wore one in March 2012 for a St. Patrick's Day parade, when she dressed appropriately in green, and later in July 2012, choosing a pale primrose creation when her husband, Prince William, was awarded the Order of the Thistle.

British-based, New Zealand-born designer Emilia Wickstead has fast become one of the go-to designers for London's high society. Despite only setting up her label in 2009, she has already dressed a number of notable clients, including Kate's cousin Lucy, fellow designer Anya Hindmarch, Lady Kitty Spencer, Emma Parker Bowles, and India Hicks, bridesmaid to the late Princess of Wales. But Wickstead's client base is not restricted to the upper echelons of the aristocracy; she can also count popstar Dannii Minogue and the British Prime Minister's fashion-forward wife Samantha Cameron as trusted customers, both of whom have worn her chic designs many times.

The Shoes and Bag To offset the dress, Kate recycled a pair of champagne-colored satin Prada pumps and a Prada clutch purse that we have seen on multiple occasions. These versatile accessories perfectly complemented the garment's pink hue.

Wear Pale Pink—without Fading into the Background!

Pink is never the easiest color to pull off, but Kate manages it with style and flair. Here's how to wear pale pink to perfection:

Keep skin tones warm
Pastel and dusky pinks can be tricky shades to wear, as their cool tones can easily drain color from your skin. But clever Kate chose to wear this soft color in early summer when she had a light tan, and also applied plenty of her signature rosy-pink blush so her complexion was a picture of glowing health.

Mix shades
Like Kate, try wearing a deeper shade of pink when it comes to your shoes and purse to offset the paleness of the dress.

Choose sumptuous fabrics
As with white, pale shades of pink look classiest in slightly heavier, more luxurious weights of fabric, so garments don't become transparent and end up looking cheap. Kate chooses wool-crepe here, but cashmere, raw silk, and felt would also work well.

Be a grown-up
Team pink with frilly styles and you risk looking far too girly. Kate avoids making this fashion faux pas by opting for an elegant, streamlined dress style that oozes restrained glamour.

Regal Recycling Kate again demonstrated her thrifty side by giving a second outing to the pricey $2,000 pink dress at her first Royal Garden Party at Buckingham Palace just two weeks later, to kickstart the Diamond Jubilee celebrations. The Royal Garden Party is a long-held annual tradition hosted by the Royal Family in celebration of those who have made a worthy contribution to public life, and they are invited for tea and cakes in the Palace grounds. It's always a special day, but this year's event was imbued with extra sentiment because it marked the Queen's 60 years on the British throne. In the same month, royal historian Sir Roy Strong claimed that the Queen herself approved of the Duchess's willingness to wear the same outfit twice, rather than always sporting something new. It is certainly something of a royal tradition, with the Queen herself having been spotted revisiting favorite outfits many times during her long reign.

The Hat When wearing the dress for the second time, Kate kept things fresh by accessorizing it with a new pink hat by Jane Corbett. The milliner shared her excitement at seeing Kate wearing her design in her blog: "Absolutely thrilled that HRH The Duchess of Cambridge chose to wear one of my hats to her first Garden Party at Buckingham Palace this afternoon," she gushed. "How wonderful!"

Emilia Wickstead

Born in New Zealand, the designer spent her formative years in Milan before graduating from Central Saint Martins College of Art and Design in London in 2007. While living in New York, Milan, and London, Emilia worked in the design studios at Giorgio Armani, Narciso Rodriguez, and Proenza Schouler, and at British *Vogue*.

She founded Emilia Wickstead in 2008 in London, with showrooms in Chelsea and Knightsbridge, and launched her flagship store in Belgravia in 2009. A ready-to-wear collection is housed in tandem with custom garments. Noted for their pretty colors, demure style, and tiny waists with pleated or A-line skirts that give a feminine, hourglass shape, the clothing is certainly "fit for a princess." Focusing on simple and sweet designs and a modern interpretation of English classics, the designs suit Kate perfectly, such as the yellow coatdress, right, worn at St. Giles Cathedral after the Thistle Ceremony on July 5, 2012, in Edinburgh, Scotland, and the belted emerald dress worn with a Lock & Co. hat for presenting St. Patrick's Day shamrocks to the Irish Guards in Aldershot, Hampshire, on March 2012, far right.

Resplendent in Royal Red

The Dress Kate wowed in this vibrant scarlet Alexander McQueen dress for one of the most spectacular events of the entire Royal Diamond Jubilee celebrations: the Thames Diamond Jubilee River Pageant on June 3, 2012. The regatta saw the largest number of boats ever assembled on the Thames in London sailing down the river, including the royal barge—*Spirit of Chartwell*—which was decorated with over 10,000 blooms, and carried HM the Queen, the Duke of Edinburgh, the Prince of Wales, the Duchess of Cornwall, the Duke and Duchess of Cambridge, and Prince Harry.

Wanting to blend in seamlessly with the most senior members of the Royal Family, Kate knew she couldn't go wrong by choosing her go-to designer for major events, Sarah Burton for Alexander McQueen. The custom-made frock incorporated multiple McQueen design elements, including the fitted dress and pleated skirt, and most resembled a wool-crepe dress from the label's Pre-Fall 2011 collection. Longer sleeves have been added and the hemline lowered to mark the formality of the occasion, while the standard boat-neck was perhaps a nod to the maritime occasion itself.

Kate has shown her affinity to this particular shade of red, wearing a "Marianne" coatdress in the same hue by Catherine Walker on the final day of her tour of Canada in 2011. Versions of this McQueen dress had also been worn by two high-profile celebrities before her: American reality TV star Kim Kardashian and U.K. *X Factor* judge and popstar Tulisa Contostavlos. But it is, of course, Kate who was credited for helping British label Alexander McQueen's U.K. and worldwide sales soar by nearly 30 percent between 2011 and 2012—a profit increase that means the label has now overtaken the sales of the previous British frontrunner, Stella McCartney.

The Brooch and Scarf Kate also wore a new brooch in the shape of two silver dolphins. It was a wedding gift from the Royal Navy Submarine Service, of which William is Commodore in Chief, and was perfectly in tune with the pageant's maritime theme. Meanwhile, Kate's cashmere scarf boasts the distinctive pattern of Strathearn tartan, and was clearly a respectful nod to the Scottish title she inherited on her marriage: the Countess of Strathearn.

The Bag and Shoes Toning perfectly with the dress, Kate's bag was a modified version of the Alexander McQueen "Classic Skull" clutch with silk bow, in which the jewel-encrusted skull (perhaps seen as inappropriate for this formal day of celebration!) was replaced with three large rhinestones. Avoiding the obvious choice of matching shoes, Kate wore her much-favored L.K. Bennett "Sledge" pumps in nude, a decision much debated by fashion commentators, but it did have the advantage of lengthening her legs and lending the dress a more summery feel.

The Hat Kate's flamboyant scarlet cocktail hat was made by Sylvia Fletcher, for royal milliner James Lock & Co, and perfectly fit the mood of the occasion. Fletcher also designed the Duchess's distinctive red maple-leaf hat worn on her tour of Canada in 2011.

Bringing a Modern Twist to Formal Occasions

Befitting the fact that she is representing a younger, more accessible breed of Royal, Kate has helped shake up formal dress protocol. In choosing edgier designers and fashion-forward accessories, she adds a fresh feel to timeless, classic pieces. Luckily, her modern style is easy to replicate without spending a fortune.

Choose skirt shapes with care
Rarely does Kate go shorter than knee-length when it comes to skirts and dresses for formal occasions, but in opting for either a classic A-line shape—or a pleated fuller shape, as at the river regatta—she creates a look that is flattering and feminine, never frumpy.

Belt up
The Duchess loves to use a belt to add shape at the waist of suit jackets and wool dresses. This lends a touch of fashion flair and sex appeal to outfits that can otherwise lack form.

Dare to flare
When Kate wears a knee-length skirt suit or dress, she often pairs it with a more modern short blazer with a slight flare or peplum, bringing the outfit up-to-date.

Shoe savvy
Matching classic outfits with modern high heels, especially with a fashionable wedge shape, means the Duchess stands out from the rest of the Royals, parading their sensible pumps. Younger women can still identify with Kate's style, too.

Stay ahead of the game
Red, blue, white, or black; lacy, feathered, or wool . . . Kate's headwear choices are wide-ranging, and it has been noted by fashion critics that no one wears a hat quite like the Duchess. Her trick is always to choose one just right for the occasion, as with this perfect red Sylvia Fletcher number at the river pageant. To mirror Kate's style, favor the smaller ornate hats or headpieces that won't cast shade over your face, and be bold with striking color choices—as long as they exactly match the key color of your outfit.

Kate Epitomizes Understated Elegance

The Dress Sarah Burton of Alexander McQueen has long been Kate's go-to designer for high-profile events, so it was no surprise when the Duchess turned up at St. Paul's Cathedral for the Jubilee Service of Thanksgiving on June 4, 2012, in a sensational custom-made dress by Burton.

It was, in fact, the third day in a row that Kate had chosen to wear an Alexander McQueen piece to the weekend of Diamond Jubilee celebrations—and she saved the best for last. The slim-fitting, nude lace shift dress has a white sheath underlay and satin waist detail. Like all the McQueen gowns that Kate favors, the dress has long sleeves, which when coupled with the knee-length hemline and boat neck, give the outfit a modest, ladylike appearance, despite its form-fitting shape.

This piece was custom-made for the Duchess by the British label, but that didn't deter copy-Kates from clamoring to re-create the look. Within hours of the Duchess arriving at the 10 a.m. service, U.K. chain Asda (owned by Walmart) reported a 35 percent rise in sales of a roughly similar nude lace dress retailing at $40, and by the end of the day, the piece was completely sold out. Never one to miss a Kate-created publicity moment, Asda brand director Fiona Lambert observed, "We expect the Kate phenomenon to continue as she has now established herself as a British style icon. We know our customers can't wait to see what she will be wearing next."

The Hat Kate's delicate beaded cocktail hat, with silk tulle, organza discs, veiling, and smoked quartz detail, was created by Jane Taylor, a Fulham-based milliner who trained under former milliner to the Queen, Marie O'Regan. It was the first time that Kate had worn one of Taylor's creations, but it wasn't the first time Taylor had created headwear for the Royal Family. Zara Phillips, Princess Eugenie, and Sophie, Countess of Wessex, have all worn her hats to official events before, and the Countess also sported one in St. Paul's that day.

"Both the Countess of Wessex and the Duchess of Cambridge look stunning," an understandably jubilant Taylor said at the time. "They both have a unique yet timeless sense of style and wear hats so well! It's a dream to have two members of the Royal Family wearing my pieces to such an important event." The milliner then went on to reveal that Kate's hat took about eight hours to make, and that the

Duchess "chose a cocktail hat because it's a happy medium between a fascinator and a more formal, bigger hat that covers the head."

The Duchess also wore the hat slightly off-center which was apparently exactly right; according to Taylor: "You should always wear hats at a jaunty angle, and Kate positions them at exactly the right angle, which makes them look flattering, and she teams them with classic outfits so they look elegant." Perhaps unsurprisingly, as soon as the Duchess was pictured wearing the hat, Taylor was bombarded with emails and orders from all around the world.

The Bag For the church occasion, Kate stuck to her favorite style of modest purse—the box clutch—and carried the Prada satin logo bag tucked neatly under her arm.

The Earrings Kate kept fashion commentators guessing about where she picked up her dazzling "diamond" and "pearl" drop earrings. So it came as a shock to many when it was revealed that they were in fact a cubic zirconia pair from independent and affordable jewelry website Heavenly Necklaces.

The company's founder, Belinda Hadden, who designed the earrings, was astonished to learn that Kate had worn her creations to such a high-profile event. It wasn't long before the "Kate Effect" began to take hold. "Within the next 24 hours, I had sold out," said Hadden. "I sold 60 on my website, which is the amount I would usually sell in a whole year. They are made of finest grade cubic zirconia, but what makes them look as authentic is the settings they are in."

The Shoes Kate mixed designer and chain store pieces with her characteristic flair by anchoring the outfit with her favorite nude L.K. Bennett "Sledge" heels. These handy heels have a small platform that cushions the toes and makes them comfortable to wear all day. At the St. Paul's service that day, Samantha Cameron, wife of British Prime Minister, David Cameron, wore the same pair of shoes—only in black!

Wear Formal Hats with Flair

A formal hat is one of the most transformative pieces you'll ever wear. It instantly adds a sense of drama to an outfit, and Kate provides a perfect lesson in how to carry one off with aplomb.

Angle it
All hats—but especially smaller, disc-shaped cocktail hats—should be worn at an angle. Kate always wears hers on the right side of her head.

Be age-appropriate
Larger hats are more suited to older women. Kate keeps her look young by choosing smaller hats that allow her to have her hair and face on display.

Limit other accessories
Remember, a hat is a dramatic statement. Don't go on to clutter your look with scarves and jewelry—opt instead for a streamlined look.

Keep hair simple
Your hairdo and your hat shouldn't be fighting for attention. By keeping her long hair in an everyday style, Kate lets her hat do all the talking.

LOOK 24

Checking Out in Style

The Dress For the launch of a new charity with Princes William and Harry on July 26, 2012 (the day before the start of the London Olympics), Kate aptly selected a simple Hobbs (a London chain store) summer dress.

The three young Royals appeared at Bacon's College in southeast London, to launch the start of their charity, the Royal Foundation—a new program that will train 16- to 19-year-olds to become qualified sports coaches and mentors. And with the Olympics just around the corner, Kate certainly took the gold medal when it came to chic summer style. The Duchess looked the picture of feminine perfection in a patterned white and gray checkered linen frock. Its classic fit and flare silhouette suited her slender frame well, and also featured a modified boatneck, short sleeves, full skirt, and a concealed back zipper.

The dress is neatly cinched to show off her tiny waist with a striking white, African-inspired braided rope belt. Somewhat predictably, the remaining dresses, which were already on sale at Hobbs for half price by the time Kate wore it, left stores in record time!

The Hair It's hard to tell from the photographs but the U.K. was in the middle of a heatwave, with temperatures of over 86°F, when Kate sported this immaculate blowout. No stranger to hot conditions following her official trips around the globe with William, the Duchess's hair remained perfectly in place, glossy and frizz-free— even when she played a quick game of soccer and refereed a judo match during the event!

The Shoes Kate finished off the look with her wallet-friendly, trusty "Imperia" wedges, from an affordable shoe chain store in London, Pied à Terre —a shoe style that has been favored by the Duchess on many other warm-weather occasions. This led fashion commentators at the *Daily Mail* newspaper to joke: "Forget the forecast, we Britons only truly know it's summer when the Duchess of Cambridge swaps her trusty L.K. Bennett 'Sledges' for a pair of Pied-à-Terre wedges." The espadrille-style wedges feature a canvas upper and buckle slingback and come in a range of colors, including "natural" as worn here by Kate.

Make Chain Store Buys Heavenly

When Kate worked as a buyer for British fashion store Jigsaw, she learned exactly how shopping in local chain stores such as Zara, Warehouse, and Hobbs results in lower-price bargains that can be made to look much more expensive. Here are some of her insider tricks:

Double up
If you find a dress or top that you love and it's a fabulous fit, do what Kate does, and purchase the piece in two or more colors—at chain store prices, you can afford to!

Diffuse your look
Shopping in chain stores doesn't have to mean giving designers a miss. An increasing number of Kate's favorite designers, such as Missoni and Alice Temperley, are extending their brands to provide a "diffusion" line— a cheaper version of their high-end fashion. Equally, some designers are now collaborating with department stores to provide catwalk-inspired pieces for a fraction of the cost, such as Karl Lagerfeld with H&M.

Be fabric savvy
You don't have to skimp on the quality of clothes just because they are cheaper. Kate loves luxe fabrics such as silk and cashmere, which you can often find in chain stores at a fraction of the cost. Cheap fabrics look and feel inferior and will deteriorate very quickly, so check the label and stick to 100 percent cotton, wool, and silk.

Think high fashion
Chain stores are exactly the right place to experiment with new-season trends, cuts, and colors. You can buy something edgy at an affordable price, which means you won't mind ditching it, if it looks dated by next year. Not that there's anything wrong with fashion recycling, of course—Kate is happy rewearing both the chain store and the designer pieces she loves.

Don't waste money on basics
As thrifty Kate knows, some basics simply aren't worth paying designer prices for. It makes sense to buy cheaper chain store versions of plain T-shirts, blouses, and even jeans, depending on how long you expect them to last. Kate, for example, chooses more expensive denim brands such as J Brand for the navy jeans she wears frequently, but when experimenting with a bright electric-blue shade, she was happy to pick some up cheaply from Zara. Mixing chain store basics with stylish accessories quickly ups the quality of your overall look.

LOOK 25

Kate's Kane and Able

The Dress For a pre-Olympic reception at Buckingham Palace in June 2012, Kate wore this striking satin coatdress, created for her by designer Christopher Kane. The formal, yet fashion-forward, frock was perfect for mingling with heads of state from all over the world, including the stylish First Lady, Michelle Obama. The single-breasted design features sharp tailoring with streamlined darts, long sleeves, slanted pockets, a belted waist, and peak lapels.

While the custom-made, ice-blue dress nodded to Kane's 2013 collection, it was in fact a softer, more demure take on the designer's edgy aesthetic, in keeping with Kate's signature style. Nevertheless, the designer, who won the New Establishment Award at the British Fashion Awards in 2011, was still an unexpected choice for the Duchess—not least to Kane himself.

Back in 2010, Scottish designer Kane had named Kate as one of the women he would love to design for and bemoaned the fact she was better known for wearing chain store pieces than for championing British designers: "It's a shame she doesn't wear more designers," he said at the time. "I don't really like the high street getting so much of the credit. I understand that there would be an array because you need to relate to so many people in the market, but she is a princess. If I were a princess, I'd be like, 'Oh yeah, bring it on!'"

Consequently, most fashion observers had written off Kane's chances of dressing the Duchess, as his pieces were considered to be too "out there" for Kate's more conservative, classic taste. But perhaps to prove that she doesn't always do the expected when it comes to style, she took up Kane's challenge and asked him to design a dress for her to wear to this very high-profile event when the world's media spotlight was sure to be focused on her outfit.

In fact, ever since the Royal Wedding, Kate's style confidence has continued to grow so that she has become far more open to experimentation when it comes to the more cutting-edge designers, trying, for example, Stella McCartney and Matthew Williamson for the first time. Perhaps most importantly, the beautiful coatdress fit her like a glove and proved to be a perfect choice for the occasion, combining fashion flair with understated elegance.

The Clutch Kate paired the coatdress with a soft gray suede clutch by Alexander McQueen. The muted tones of the bag provide a great textural counterpoint to her shimmering dress.

McQueen's clutches usually feature a bold skull clasp. However, like Kate's dress, this piece was customized to work with her style, and the skull clasp was replaced with a simpler clasp. The fact that such high-profile designers are willing to alter their key pieces for Kate is further proof of how much sway she has over the fashion world.

The Earrings The Duchess's blue topaz and diamond earrings are by one of her favorite jewelry designers, Kiki McDonough. The hooped earrings have an open circle composed of 11 oval topazes, which graduate in size from top to bottom, creating an eye-catching effect.

Wearing Satin with Style

Satin is not a forgiving fabric. A badly made or poor-fitting piece in this shiny material is a glaringly obvious fashion disaster, which can make even the slimmest figure bulge in the wrong places. Yet Kate, as always, carries off this difficult look with ease, by following some important rules.

Fit is foremost
Any places in which the satin is pulled taut will be unflatteringly highlighted by the shiny fabric; even though Kate doesn't shy away from form-fitting numbers, on this occasion her dress is a little looser than usual. By opting for a more relaxed fit, she avoids any unwanted tight spots in the fabric. Sadly, most of us cannot buy custom so, if in doubt, go for a size up.

Keep it sleek
Excess fabric and swooshing A-line skirts can look bridal when cut in satin. Opt for sharp, tailored lines like Kate's coatdress to keep the look sophisticated and occasion-appropriate. Always ensure satin is perfectly pressed to avoid unflattering folds or creases.

Change it up
By going for a coatdress rather than her classic shift or sheath-style dress, Kate cleverly mixes masculine tailoring with feminine fabric, preventing the look from becoming prissy.

Consider what lies beneath
Choice of underwear is also very important when wearing satin, and Kate would never dream of being spotted with something so vulgar as a VPL (visible panty line). Invest in a set of flesh-colored seamless panties and bra to avoid satin draping awkwardly over lacy lingerie or bulky seams.

LOOK 26

Stylish Olympic Spirit

The Dress While cheering on Andy Murray at the Olympic Men's Singles Quarter-finals on August 2, 2012, Kate wore a Stella McCartney "Ridley Stretch Cady" dress, which she'd previously worn to an Olympics exhibition at London's National Portrait Gallery, just two weeks earlier. This simple crepe shift embodies classic luxury with its figure-hugging minimalist silhouette and eye-catching royal blue hue.

McCartney was also the British designer chosen to create the official Olympic uniform for Team GB for London 2012, so the dress made a perfect choice for the team's most photographed supporter. For her Olympic uniform, McCartney famously played down the red of the traditional Union Jack flag and instead accented the blue—"something that was very important to me was to try and use that very iconic image but to dismantle it and try to soften it, break it down, and make it more fashionable in a sense," said the designer at the time. Kate is so cute with fashion that it is probably no coincidence that she was seen sporting a bold blue Stella McCartney for two key Olympic events. With this smart color choice, she proudly shows her support for the British designer and her patriotic solidarity with the British athletes, wearing McCartney's blue outfits.

Kate and Prince William also caused a stir on this occasion in choosing to sit among the crowd instead of using Wimbledon's famous Royal Box. Foregoing special privileges at an important event is another clear signal that the couple want to be seen as very non-traditional—a couple who can mix formal and informal, and enjoy themselves, whatever the surroundings.

The Blazer Kate topped her dress with a tailored, one-button blazer from the Canadian label Smythe Les Vestes. Known for their perfectly tailored and sartorially savvy blazers, Smythe has a strong cult following among celebrities and fashion editors alike. The blazer's bold gold buttons, large lapels, masculine tailoring, and cutout back panel give this classic item a contemporary flair.

It was, in fact, the third time Kate wore this navy blazer to Olympic events in one week, but then the Duchess has made an art of picking versatile pieces, in classic shapes, that work perfectly with the rest of her wardrobe to create a number of different looks. It is this knack of selecting pieces that can be used in multiple ways that has earned Kate the title "Queen of the Capsule Wardrobe" among some of her adoring fashion press.

The Clutch Kate matched her navy blazer with a navy suede "Muse" clutch bag from Russell & Bromley. The piece was designed by Stuart Weitzman, another favorite of the Duchess when it comes to accessories, and a label that also counts both singer Beyoncé and actress Angelina Jolie as fans.

The Shoes Another clear favorite during the Olympics were the Stuart Weitzman "Coco Pop" shoes. The fact that this comfortable pair hardly left the Duchess's feet during the Games was not lost on Weitzman. "She didn't change her shoes for nine days. It was a big deal!" he delightedly observed. Predictably, the Coco Pop's stacked style became an instant hit.

The Sunglasses Throughout the tense match, Kate protected her eyes from the sunlight with a pair of sleek Givenchy SGV 761 sunglasses. Featuring broad arms and rectangular frames, the glasses oozed simple French chic.

Speak Volumes with Your Fashion Choices

Don't be fooled by her effortlessly stylish appearance, Kate puts an incredible amount of thought into everything she wears. Even a seemingly simple outfit such as her vibrant blue dress and navy blazer combo actually makes a discrete statement about the event she is attending. In paying attention to these key details, Kate ensures her outfit is always on point.

Match your designer to your destination Think about where you've bought your clothes. Picking a piece by a designer who has ties with the event or the location that you will be visiting, as Kate has done with her McCartney dress, is a cute sartorial nod that won't be lost on seasoned fashion-watchers.

Symbolize with accessories

You don't have to wear official or sponsored pieces to show your support for an event. Think outside the box and look for accessories that play on themes of the day. Kate first paired her McCartney dress with a circular pendant necklace by Cartier, and often sported her circular Kiki McDonough earrings during her appearances at the Games, choices that cleverly played on the Olympic Rings in a high-fashion way.

Insider jokes

Kate loves making clever sartorial statements, which only true fashion insiders will notice. Another example of this is on Look 15 (see page 73) when Kate wore shoes named after a type of daffodil for St. David's Day. These little details are the sign of a true fashionista, who thinks about what she wears and is confident enough to let her outfits do the talking.

Show your true colors

Throughout the Olympics, Kate dressed in blue, paying homage to the uniforms of her home team.

LOOK 27

Flying the Flag for British Fashion

The Dress For her appearance at the London 2012 Olympic Games Closing Ceremony on August 12, 2012, Kate chose to wear the same dress she had worn to the Diamond Jubilee Concert in June. It was fitting, and typically clever, for the Duchess to tie together the two events that effectively served as the bookends for what was an especially golden summer for the U.K.

The long-sleeved bodycon dress is from one of Kate's favorite chain store brands, Whistles. Although the so-called "Bella" dress may have been off the rack, it could have been designed especially for Kate, as it perfectly fits not only her slender frame but also her signature demure style. The aqua coloring was a great way to round off Kate's Olympic run of "blue outfits," while the multi-petal print provides a fun edge—perfect for such a jubilant occasion. She chose to accentuate the dress's flattering cinched waist and ruching detail with the addition of a thin black belt.

Kate has become something of an unofficial ambassador for the Whistles label, with her support of the brand causing the company website to crash when avid followers frantically fought to log on! But even Whistles, which had plenty of previous experience of the "Kate Effect", were surprised by just how huge the response was to this global televised event. "The biggest impact has been on a dress she wore at the Closing Ceremony," confirmed Jane Shepherdson, chief executive of Whistles: "It's a style that's been very successful for us anyway—a printed silk dress. That weekend, we sold out of it."

The Olympics Closing Ceremony celebrated home-grown talent, from sporting to artistic, including a segment featuring famous British models such as Kate Moss, Lily Cole, and Naomi Campbell in extravagant outfits from British designers, including Erdem, Victoria Beckham, and Alexander McQueen. Kate is always happy to fly the flag for British fashion, and her made-in-Britain outfit was perfect in keeping with the theme of the occasion, while also juxtaposing the show's couture fashion with more accessible pieces.

The Earrings As at the Diamond Jubilee Concert, Kate echoed the color of her dress with blue topaz and diamond earrings by Kiki McDonough, the same pair she wore in June. These circular earrings cleverly pick up on the design of the Olympic rings, a little fashion joke that explains why Kate wore this pair to so many of her Olympic appearances.

The Arm Candy Kate completed this recycled outfit with her trusty white gold Tiffany "Diamond's by the Yard" bracelet and her Anya Hindmarch "Maud" clutch. Crafted of soft satin and made using tightly woven thread, the black clutch has a luxurious glossy appearance.

Dressing Up Buys

While designer pieces were being flaunted during the Closing Ceremony, Kate ensured her Whistles dress held its own amid all the finery by using some simple style tricks.

Add embellishments
Designer pieces tend to have more detail than chain store pieces but by simply wearing a slim black belt with her dress, Kate adds another note of visual interest.

Savvy sizing
Don't always stick to the same-size clothing. Pick pieces that fit you like a glove, no matter what the size says on the label, and you'll look as if it was especially made for you. Searching for the perfect fit, rather than an ideal size, ensures Kate's Whistles dress looks every bit as special as the pieces that she has custom-made.

Wear striking jewelry
Kate's pretty earrings caught the light whenever she moved her head, adding a little edge and flair to an otherwise simple outfit.

Pick a print
The right print can add a twist to any outfit and can also have the effect of making a piece appear more expensive. The tight-petal print on the Whistles dress is more impressionistic than classic floral and, consequently, brings the look up-to-date.

A Rare and Exotic Bloom

The Dress When Kate and Prince William arrived in Singapore on September 12, 2012, for a visit to the island's Botanical Gardens on the first day of their royal tour of Southeast Asia and the South Pacific, all eyes were drawn to the Duchess's exquisite pastel-pink, kimono-style dress. The royal couple were there to see the *Vanda* William Catherine orchid, a newly created orchid named in their honor. And what better way to dress for this special occasion than by choosing a special orchid-print dress?

The stunning silk dress, made for Kate by British designer Jenny Packham, was covered in tiny orchids, which took a team of skilled artists at the firm of de Gournay in London eight weeks to hand paint. The knee-grazing number also had three-quarter sleeves, a deep V-neck, and a full skirt, and was cinched in at the waist to hug Kate's delicate contours. "She looked beautiful and we are all very proud," the team at Packham declared. Even Prince William himself remarked that the colors of the hybrid *Vanda* William Catherine orchid perfectly matched the Duchess's dress—another example of Kate's amazing attention to detail when selecting an outfit.

Jenny Packham does not sell any of the designs she has made especially for the Duchess, frustrating Kate's most avid fashion followers, but this ensures that the custom outfits remain special. "We're not Reiss," explained Packham in a good-humored aside. The designer's flagship boutique, on the site of a former bank in Mayfair, London, is visited by only a privileged few, and feels exclusive. The extremely private dressing room, where clients, including Kate Winslet, Elizabeth Hurley, and Angelina Jolie, slip on their custom clothes, is a windowless space inside a former vault.

While visiting the gardens, Kate and William were also shown a white orchid, named after William's late mother, Diana. The Princess of Wales had been delighted to have a flower named in her honor, but tragically died in a Paris car crash just two weeks before she was due to fly out to see it for herself.

The Shoes and Bag Instead of her usual nude heels, Kate sported a pair of off-white "Park Avenue" pumps from Russell & Bromley, and carried a matching "Park Avenue" clutch. Although nude-toned shoes would have worked well with this dress, after a 14-hour flight, head-to-toe flesh tones might have caused Kate to look washed-out, whereas

Vanda William Catherine

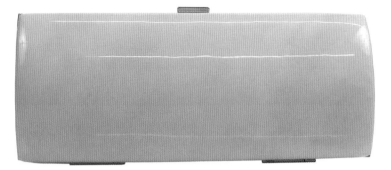

her off-white shoes picked up on the off-white detailing in the floral dress and helped to ensure the Duchess looked as fresh as a daisy.

The Earrings Kate's 18-carat gold earrings are "Classic Baroque Pearl Earring Drops" from Annoushka Jewellery, the eponymous line from Annoushka Ducas, who also founded another of Kate's go-to jewelry collections, Links of London, in the 1990s. "I am so thrilled to see the Duchess of Cambridge wearing my favorite pearl drop earrings on so many occasions," said Ducas.

The Hair Kate might have just endured a long flight before visiting the Botanical Gardens, but her hair showed no sign of fatigue! As always, her glossy locks looked perfectly groomed—neatly pinned back at the sides and front, but worn loose in cascading curls at the back. Taking some of the credit for this was Amanda Cook Tucker, the new hairstylist Kate took along with her for this official tour of Southeast Asia. Cook Tucker has cut William and Harry's hair since they were children and while Kate still goes to Richard Ward's salon in London, she occasionally likes to have her hair done at home and to have a stylist who will happily travel abroad. Cook Tucker proved indispensable on this trip, during which Kate had to contend with the implacable enemy of smooth hair—hot, humid weather. But Palace insiders were quick to reveal that the British taxpayer wasn't footing this particular grooming bill. Instead, the Prince of Wales paid the hairdresser's estimated $500-a-day fees plus travel costs.

Capture a Sense of Occasion in Your Clothes

Kate's clothes don't just match her shoes, they match the occasion, too. Here's how you can capture the essence of an event in your own outfits:

Highlight the key detail

With her specially created orchid-print dress, Kate is paying homage to the reason for her visit to Singapore's Botanical Gardens. She could have settled for a floral pattern but by going one step further and selecting an orchid pattern in the same shade as the flower named after her, she really captures the spirit of the event.

Pay respect to your hosts

If the pattern pays tribute to the flower, the oriental style of Kate's dress is a respectful nod to Singapore's fashion history and to the influence it has had on designers around the world.

Keeping the fairytale alive

The neckline and sleeves of this dress were similar to Kate's famous Alexander McQueen wedding gown. By picking up details from such an important dress, Kate is carefully crafting her own personal fashion narrative and placing the newly created orchid inside her own romantic history.

Kate Goes Graphic

The Dress She may love home-grown talent, but Kate proved she had a finger on the international fashion pulse when she stepped out in this eye-catching yet elegant dress by Singapore-born designer Prabal Gurung, to attend a state dinner hosted by the President of Singapore, on September 11, 2012.

The unusual purple and cream floral-printed wool-silk dress, from the designer's Spring/Summer 2012 collection, was inspired by a series of photographs titled "Sensual Flowers" by the renowned Japanese artist Nobuyoshi Araki. Prints were arranged symmetrically down the front of the dresses, with the reverse patterns matching up in an undulating design. Kate's dress is knee-length, with a bateau neckline, three-quarter sleeves, a concealed zipper, and a classic shift silhouette.

Since launching his label in New York in 2009, Gurung has gathered a long list of celebrity clients, including Michelle Obama and Sarah Jessica Parker, yet he was very excited when he learned that the Duchess of Cambridge was wearing one of his pieces, especially in his home country of Singapore. "This is the ultimate honor," he declared. "I had been hoping that she would wear one of our dresses but for it to happen while she's visiting the part of the world I was born in and right in the midst of New York Fashion Week is an absolute dream come true."

The designer also took to Twitter to express his joy, telling his followers how he was so excited that he "stopped some strangers on the street" to show them a picture of "Kate Middleton in our dress!"

The Accessories It's not the first time that Kate let her bold choice of dress do all the talking, finishing off her look with a selection of accessories that she has been seen with many times before: her Anya Hindmarch "Maud" clutch, black Prada satin heels, and a glittering diamond bracelet, believed to have been a wedding present and which she previously wore to a BAFTA dinner (see also page 63).

Grab Attention in Graphic Prints

If you're undecided about donning a "look-at-me" print, follow these tips for pulling off bold fabric designs with all the classical elegance of Kate.

Rule of thumb
Small, intricate prints are better for making you appear smaller, while larger patterns usually make you look, well, larger.

Balance it out
When wearing a graphic print dress, keep accessories neutral, and hair and makeup clean and simple, to avoid the look becoming too busy.

Focus attention where you want it
Remember, eyes will be drawn to bold prints, so think carefully about their placement. If you have a boyish frame, go for prints that fall on the bust and hips, and if you are curvier, look for prints that draw the eye to the center of the outfit.

Be sensible with shapes
The sleek, sophisticated shape of Kate's classic shift ensures her overall look is chic and not gaudy.

LOOK 30

Kate Pays Her Respects

The Dress Kate wore another custom Jenny Packham creation when she and Prince William paid a visit to Singapore's Kranji War Memorial, which bears the names of more than 24,000 Commonwealth casualties from World War II.

At the foot of the memorial, the royal couple laid a beautiful wreath of red roses, white lilies, and orchids on behalf of the Queen and Prince Philip, with the accompanying message: "In Memory of the Glorious Dead, Elizabeth R and Philip."

Fitting for the solemn occasion on which she was representing HM the Queen herself, Kate's dress was a soft, tranquil color—the same "duck-egg blue" shade that featured heavily in Jenny Packham's Spring/Summer 2011 collection. However, as with all Packham's creations for the Duchess, this graceful shirt dress, featuring three-quarter-length sleeves, button-front bodice, lace overlay, cinched waist, and pleated knee-length skirt, was custom-made to suit the Duchess's signature look.

The Shoes A visit to a cemetery is not an occasion for look-at-me shoes and once again Kate put her trust in her nude patent L.K. Bennett "Sledge" pumps. She may have faced some criticism for wearing the same pair of shoes on so many different occasions but her knack for creating clever capsule collections for foreign trips is built on versatile pieces that can be mixed and matched. Few items work as hard as these shoes—the perfect neutral anchor for a great variety of colorful outfits.

The Parasol Keeping accessories to a bare minimum for this somber event, Kate chose to protect her skin and hair from the midday heat with a paper parasol. Despite looking fittingly Far Eastern, she had actually bought it from a small family-run business based in East Calder, Scotland.

Christine Naysmith runs Brolliesgalore with her mom Linda, and they have been selling custom umbrellas online since 2003. They received a surprising call for a rush order on the paper and bamboo "Sa" parasol just before Kate left for the Orient.

"I couldn't believe it when I picked up the phone and it was a girl from Clarence House, asking about the parasol," recalled Christine excitedly. "She wanted the cream-colored one and explained it was for the Duchess and she needed it quickly because she was going on tour, so we had it sent by courier."

The family received an even bigger shock when their creation appeared on the news. "I was cooking tea when my daughter Christine shouted me through from the front room and the Duchess was on the TV, holding our umbrella," mom Linda explained. "Everyone was jumping up and down and we phoned everyone that works for us."

The cause of all this celebration is a delicate white paper parasol with panels handmade from the bark of the mulberry tree, and a 24-inch (60-cm) bamboo stem with a carved handle made from sustainable wood.

Look Pretty in Pleats

For many women, pleats bring back memories of unflattering school uniforms, but pleated skirts have become one of Kate's fail-safe style choices. She has modeled versions from designers including Jenny Packham, Alexander McQueen, and Jaeger, and somehow her classic look and perfect posture ensure they always appear sophisticated and chic. Here's how to follow her lead in pleats:

Look out for length
Too short and you'll look like a schoolgirl, too long and you'll appear matronly. Kate gets it just right by picking skirts that fall on, or just above, the knee.

Smooth lines
Too tight and the pleats won't fall right, and will look messy and uneven. For a more flattering effect, pleats should lie flat. If you have curvy hips and thighs, don't bypass a pleated skirt; just look for skinny "accordion" pleats—thin pleats are more elongating.

Lighten up
Pleats made out of thick, heavy fabric can add excess volume to your lower half and make you look frumpy. However, lighter fabrics have none of this heaviness and stiffness—instead, they lightly skim the body, creating a delicate sense of fullness.

Perfect proportions
High-waisted full pleats, as featured in Kate's Jenny Packham frock, add a couple of extra inches to your lower half and will balance out the volume of the skirt to create a flattering, leg-lengthening effect.

Modest Mosque Magic

The Dress A visit to a mosque, complete with rigid dress code, is an engagement that could trip up many fashionistas, but Kate appeared cool, calm, and collected in this pretty pale mint Beulah London "Sabitri" dress and matching headscarf when she and William arrived at the As Syakirin Mosque in Kuala Lumpur on September 14, 2012.

The Duchess had clearly put a lot of time and thought into her choice of clothing for such a culturally sensitive occasion and settled on this respectful, but still beautiful silk chiffon combination. In covering her hair and arms and wearing a below-the-knee dress, Kate displayed full respect for Islamic religious protocols, yet the dress offered a shapely silhouette. Demure but distinctly feminine, the soft hue shades perfectly suited her brunette coloring, too.

Royal commentators were quick to point out that this highly appropriate outfit evoked memories of Princess Diana, who displayed similar fashion savvy on multiple royal visits to mosques. In particular, Kate's late mother-in-law appeared in a very similar outfit on a visit to a mosque during a tour of Egypt in 1992.

The Duchess's choice of designer was Beulah London, a label she has previously worn—including stepping out in their coral and white flower-patterned "Blossom" dress for a friend's Somerset wedding in June 2012. This particular dress is actually a custom version of the same "Blossom" design, with an almost identical shape and cut. Ethical fashion brand Beulah London is owned by a friend of Kate and William, Lady Natasha Rufus Isaacs, and is dedicated to social justice, including employing former victims of Indian human trafficking to help manufacture clothing and accessories.

Founded in 2011, the brand has already won many high-profile customers, including Kate Moss, Sienna Miller, Sarah Jessica Parker and Demi Moore. And yet this much-photographed occasion was perhaps Beulah London's largest showcase so far. The morning after the Duchess wore this pretty dress, the label was inundated with requests from women all over the world, desperate to get their hands on it. Only Kate could transform what was a sensitive diplomatic visit into fashion frenzy, without ever looking like she was trying too hard.

The Bag Kate's clutch was the suitably modest and also much-loved beige L.K. Bennett "Natalie", which made regular appearances on the 2011 royal tour of Canada and has continued to be a versatile favorite.

The Shoes Kate wore her ever-faithful L.K. Bennett nude "Sledge" pumps with this pale dress but, in accordance with Islamic practices, she removed her shoes to enter the mosque, revealing the trademark nude pantyhose she was wearing underneath. A keen observer of important details, her toenails were not painted, as it is deemed inappropriate for a woman to wear nail polish when entering a mosque.

Be Bold with Your Brows

Wearing a headscarf was, of course, part of the dress code for the mosque, but on this particular occasion it drew even more attention to Kate's face and her choice of tastefully natural makeup. It also made a feature of her perfectly groomed eyebrows. Kate's straight, full, defined brows have become something of a trademark look for the Duchess and she has been credited with starting a new trend for bolder, bushier shapes, as opposed to very thin or arched styles. Here's how you, too, can achieve statement brows that frame your face in the most flattering way.

Establish a good base shape
Brows should start in line with the corner of your eye. To figure out where they should finish, line up a makeup brush at a diagonal angle running from the corner of your nose along the outside of your iris as you look forward. Your brow should end at the point crossing the line of the brush.

Fake the fullness
Kate's secret weapon is reported to be Bobbi Brown eyeshadow powder in sable. Use a slanted eyeshadow brush to apply a color two shades darker than your hair to fill in any gaps in your brows.

Try a dye job
Having your eyebrows professionally dyed at a beauty salon is a great way to add Kate-style definition.

Keep them neat
Kate's brows never have a hair out of place. Use an eyebrow brush or a clean mascara brush to groom unruly hairs into shape, and set them with a slick of Vaseline.

Kate's Malaysian Marvel

The Dress Glittering in gold and soft white, Kate dazzled in a floor-length Alexander McQueen gown as she attended a lavish dinner thrown by the Malaysian head of state, Sultan Abdul Halim of Kedah, at the opulent Istana Negara state palace in Kuala Lumpur.

The dress featured a fitted bodice and a flared skirt, which flowed out from the empire waistline, with gold lamé embroidery bordering the sleeves, neck, and center of the gown. Her sweetheart neckline caused some murmurs from onlookers as to its appropriateness in a conservative country, however Kate kept the tops of her arms covered and wore a floor-skimming skirt in line with local protocol.

As with Kate's custom pieces, there is more to this creation than first meets the eye: scattered over the fabric was glittering gold lamé embroidery in a hibiscus motif. The hibiscus is the official flower of Malaysia, making this subtle design detail another example of the Duchess's canny ability to pay homage to her host country through her choice of outfit.

The Jewelry Kate picked up on the hibiscus print of her dress with her leaf-shaped gold jewelry. The "Double Leaf" earrings and matching "Spread Your Wings" bracelet are by designer Catherine Zoraida, who is known for her exquisitely handcrafted pieces. Born in Colombia, but raised in Scotland, Zoraida says she combines the influences of both countries in her nature-inspired designs. Featuring beautifully engraved feather details, both of these gold-plated silver items were handmade in England.

The Duchess picked out the pieces from the website myflashtrash.com, a jewelry store founded by *Made in Chelsea* TV star Amber Atherton. The company's head of public relations, Abbey Keys, commented: "Kate can't

accept gifting, so for our designers it's a lovely feeling to know that she has chosen these pieces because she genuinely likes them, instead of just wearing them because they were a gift."

The Bag The clutch carried by Kate is one that she has used for many formal events, as has her sister Pippa, who owns a matching one. The shiny gold purse, with a dramatic jewel-encrusted brooch clasp, is from Wilbur & Gussie—a label founded by childhood friends Brett Tyne and Lucy Lyons. "Wilbur and Gussie were our family pets when we were growing up, and therefore integral parts of our childhood," they explained. "Naming our business proved to be no easy task, until we came up with the idea to incorporate their names. Regal mongrel cat Wilbur reflects what's elegant and refined about us, and Gussie, the strong-minded Westie dog, mirrors what's bold and occasionally off-the-wall."

Interest in the then relatively unknown brand's "Charlie" clutch purse rocketed when the Duchess of Cambridge was pictured carrying the glittering envelope design. The bag itself is also named after a pet—a blue Burmese cat. "He's a bit of a show-stopper due to his striking good looks, but not inherently an attention-seeker," they explained. "He's quietly confident and head-turningly handsome."

The Shoes Just peeping out from the bottom of Kate's skirt were Jimmy Choo "Dart Glitter" sandals in gold. They may be hidden but the high heels and platforms on these shoes helped balance out the proportions of Kate's floor-length gown and gave her the necessary added height to carry off such a flowing shape.

Pick Out a Show-stopping Outfit

The eyes of the fashion world are always on Kate—even when she's just in a sweater and jeans. Yet she still knows how to pull out all the stops and wow a crowd when a more formal occasion calls for it. Here's how she does it:

Step out of your comfort zone
Kate usually wears shift dresses to formal events, with waists that fall on the natural waistline. In going for a full-length empire-cut gown, so markedly different from her normal choices, she knows that she will set tongues wagging for all the right reasons.

Go for gold
Train the spotlight on yourself by wearing metallics. They glitter and shine in the evening lights, and instantly add drama and sparkle.

Create a dramatic silhouette
Whether it's a billowing ballgown or an elaborate bell-shaped sleeve, creating a striking silhouette ensures you will stand out from the crowd and look dramatic in photos.

Play with proportion
The empire cut of Kate's dress makes it look as if she has legs that literally go all the way up to her armpits! A grand occasion such as this is the perfect opportunity to display your best assets to the max.

OPPOSITE: It had been rumored that the Duchess of Cambridge would wear a tiara for this official state dinner at Istana Negara Palace in Kuala Lumpur, but she chose to keep things simple instead. Her brunette locks were partially pulled back and up at the sides and front, then loosely twisted into place at the back, with the rest of her long hair falling in a soft waterfall of cascading curls.

A Vision of Grace in Lace

The Dress When she attended the Diamond Jubilee tea party hosted by the British High Commissioner at his residence in Kuala Lumpur on September 14, 2012, Kate chose to wear this delightful ice-blue dress with white lace overlay by one of her all-time favorite British designers, Alice Temperley. Lace is, of course, the perfect choice for afternoon tea, and Kate looked cool and chic in the outfit, despite this marking what must have been one of the most difficult days for the Duchess of Cambridge since she first became a public figure. That same morning, she had been informed that unauthorized pictures of her sunbathing while topless on vacation had been published by the French magazine *Closer*. And yet this emerging scandal didn't prevent unflappable Kate from looking calm and elegant and smiling charmingly for the waiting photographers.

Her knee-length dress with three-quarter sheer sleeves, a boat neckline and flared skirt is a modified version of the "Aster Flower Dress" from Temperley London's Fall/Winter 2012 collection. The original frock came in black silk with a gold overlay, but the designer created this pale blue and white version especially for Kate, as the lighter palette was more fitting for the tropical climate on her royal tour of South-East Asia and the South Pacific.

Alice Temperley has seen her designs worn by both Middleton sisters, a boost that is not lost on the designer.

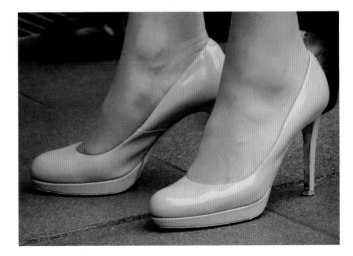

"Awareness is good for any brand," she has admitted. "They're wonderful girls to dress and wonderful girls to be around, so I think it's all flattering." The Somerset-born designer also said of Kate: "She's been brilliant for British fashion and great for the whole economy. There is no one else who has an effect like her. It has really brought British fashion to the forefront again. She is a breath of fresh air and has encouraged people to experiment and combine high fashion with high-street fashion. She is a really nice girl as well."

The Hairpins Kate wore her hair in an elaborate braided chignon decorated with pearl pins. The style was another subtle nod of respect to the culture of her host country, as Malay women frequently wear pearl pins in their hair, especially at weddings.

The Shoes Once again, Kate's feet were cushioned in her trusty nude L.K. Bennett "Sledge" pumps.

The Earrings The Duchess's earrings, by an unnamed designer, comprised a line of five diamonds from which suspended a teardrop consisting of a large blue stone encircled by more diamonds.

ABOVE: As exemplified in this picture, Kate, who prefers to do her own makeup, has become a master at cleverly defining her eyes. One of her secrets is that she often uses navy or dark brown mascara rather than jet black, to create a softer look. She is also never seen without eyeliner, usually lining the whole eye but, again to avoid a harsh finish, she tends to choose charcoal gray or dark brown rather than black.

Wear Lace Well

Kate is clearly a huge fan of lace designs. In fact, ever since she chose a wedding dress featuring a bodice of French Chantilly lace and English Cluny lace, the Duchess has returned to the fabric for many of her public appearances. If a collection of one of Kate's favorite designers, from Erdem to Temperley, features a lace dress, you can be sure she will snap up a version of it. But it can still be a tricky fabric to wear well, so here's how to ensure you look elegant and ladylike in lace:

Tailoring and lace combination
Sharp, tailored shapes are the perfect counterbalance to lace's whimsical flimsiness. Keeping edges clean, as seen in Kate's Alexander McQueen shift featured in Look 23 (see page 100), prevents lace from appearing tacky.

Experiment with colors
The delicate, sheer nature of the fabric means you can get away with wearing lace in colors that you may usually find draining, especially if there is a contrasting or deeper-colored underlay fabric.

Don't slip up
Lace creates an effect that is subtly sexy. Keep the look classy, not trashy, by ensuring you wear a full slip underneath. A VPL (visible panty line) and visible bra straps are so unladylike!

Too much of a good thing
One lace piece is enough! Matching a lace dress with a lace shawl, gloves, or other accessories is simply overkill.

Let lower layers shine through
Experiment with different color slips underneath a lace top or dress to create entirely different outfits. Soft pastel colors, as in Kate's Temperley dress, play up to the pretty romantic nature of the fabric, while bright, jewel colors underneath can create a more dramatic, gothic effect.

LOOK 34

Aussie Fashion Rules

The Dress It is surely no coincidence that the first time Kate stepped foot on Australian soil was also the first time she wore a piece by the Project D label. Although the brand is based in London, the more famous half of the designer duo behind it is Aussie popstar Dannii Minogue. She set up the label with her best friend, Tabitha Somerset Webb, in 2010. In just a few short years, Project D has gained popularity for its range of gorgeous frocks, including chic cocktail dresses, red-carpet glamour gowns, and super-stylish day numbers.

Kate wore the "Penelope" dress in pale powder-pink from Project D's Spring/Summer 2012 collection, which features a fold-down collar, cuffed short sleeves, box-pleated skirt, waist tie, thin belt loops, and an invisible zipper on the front. The simple tea dress was made out of lightweight silk crepe de Chine, making it well suited to the climate of both the Polynesian island Tuvalu, from where the couple flew, and Brisbane, Australia, where they landed.

Kate's sister, Pippa Middleton, had previously worn a Project D "Phoebe Bluebird Peplum" dress back in July of the same year to watch tennis at Wimbledon, but it was when the Duchess was snapped in the "Penelope" dress that the small-scale brand, with a total staff of just 11, was suddenly front-page news. "I was getting onto a flight back to Australia, just about to turn off my phone when a text came through saying she was wearing one of our dresses," recalled an elated Dannii Minogue. "There are actually only four left now on the rack in the office."

Getting Kate into one of their girlie, sassy frocks was a personal victory for Minogue, who had confessed to reporters back in March: "There's probably not a brand in town that wouldn't want to dress the Duchess of Cambridge. She's an iconic, gorgeous girl and if she ever chose to wear Project D, we would be incredibly proud."

The Shoes During their journey back to the U.K. from the Far East on September 19, 2012, the Duke and Duchess of Cambridge had a two-hour layover at Brisbane Airport, and Kate ensured she was comfortable for the occasion by slipping into her well-worn L.K. Bennett nude "Sledge" pumps.

The Earrings Kate also chose this occasion to showcase a new pair of earrings—the 24-carat gold-plated disc stud earrings with a pale blue amazonite. The brand is called Azuni and it is widely available from British department store John Lewis.

Azuni's founder and designer, Ashley Marshall, actually began his career as a chef, working in some of London's top kitchens, such as the Dorchester hotel, the Ivy and Le Caprice, before spending time living in South America, where he picked up the cultural influences clearly seen in his work. Marshall likes to experiment with unusual textures and stones to create jewelry that sits "Between Two Worlds", such as these antique-style earrings.

OPPOSITE: When leaving the Polynesian island Tuvalu to head back to Britain, Kate and Prince William were taken to their plane on a throne lifted by local men, escorted by colorful dancers, and were presented with these traditional floral head garlands. As always, Kate anticipates this honor by wearing a silk flower-print Project D dress that perfectly complements the flower "crown," known locally as a *fou*.

Picking the Right Celebrity Designers

Kate may be a fan of Danni Minogue's label Project D, but she is picky about which celebrity designers receive the royal seal of approval. Here is how she always makes the right decision:

Choose for yourself
Recently, Kate returned a collection of clothes sent to her from the line created for U.K. shop Dorothy Perkins by the Kardashian sisters. A representative of the Duchess noted at the time: "In general terms, the policy of the Duke and Duchess of Cambridge is not to accept any unsolicited gifts unless the sender is known personally to His or Her Royal Highness. Any such gifts are returned to the sender with thanks and an explanation of Their Royal Highnesses' policy."

Stick to your signature style
Although Kate cannot accept gifts, if there had been a piece in the Kardashian collection that caught her eye, she would probably have bought it. But the racy collection featuring a lot of animal prints—which Dorothy Perkins dubbed the Kardashians' "look at me" red-carpet glamour—is a far cry from Kate's more demure, classic style.

Try before you buy
Just because you admire a celebrity's personal style doesn't mean their clothes will work on you. Kate asked to be sent a selection from Victoria Beckham's highly successful Spring/Summer 2011 collection, as favored by many Hollywood A-listers. However, to date, she has never worn anything from the line, suggesting that after trying on the off-the-rack pieces, she decided they simply didn't work for her.

Keeping Out the Cold

The Coat For the opening of the soccer park St. George's, the Football Association's new National Football Centre in Staffordshire, England, on October 9, 2012, Kate wore this "Angel Fit and Flare" coat in a flattering shade of khaki-green from her much-favored British brand Reiss.

The wool coat, from the Reiss Fall/Winter 2010 collection, is very much aligned with Kate's signature look: elegant tailoring, which nips in at the waist before flaring out into a full skirt. The knee-length coat also features large cuffs, a hidden front fastening and a wide funnel collar, which can be turned up (as Kate did) or worn folded down.

The popular store first opened in 1971 and, in more recent years, has gained a reputation for design-led clothing that is especially popular with young, city-based professionals who want affordable fashion with a bit of catwalk edge. The brand has been one of the few British retailers to crack the American market after opening its first store in Greenwich Village, New York, in 2005.

Kate actually purchased her coat from the Reiss outlet store, which sells surplus stock from previous collections at cheaper prices and is based at her favorite bargain shopping outlet: Bicester Village. Kate had previously worn this classy coat on Christmas Day 2011, when on her way to a church service with the Princesses Beatrice and Eugenie.

The Belt Kate ensured her simple coat looked dressed up enough for the formal occasion with the addition of a statement belt that cinched the coat in extra-tight at the waist. The black patent mock-croc "Betony" belt is also from Reiss, but from their 2009 collection. In mixing and matching pieces from different seasons, Kate is showing off another aspect of her keen fashion eye, creating timeless looks from favorite saved pieces, rather than blindly following current seasonal trends.

The Boots Kate picked her favorite boots—the Aquatalia "Rhumba"—and teamed them with opaque black pantyhose. It's not always advisable to wear heels on grass, but the low heel didn't cause her any problems. Although the weatherproofed suede and slip-resistant rubber sole proved suitable attire for the event, sporty Kate still joked about slipping into something more suitable for a soccer game.

Belt Up!—the Five Belts Every Girl Needs

Kate is a dedicated fan of belts and has a collection of classic styles that she uses to alter many different outfits. With just a handful of belts at your disposal, you can transform the look of simple dresses, coats, and top-and-skirt combinations. Your essential belt collection should consist of the following:

The skinny belt
Perfect for drawing the eye to the narrowest point on your figure, skinny belts look best worn with delicate fabrics, such as lace or fine knits. They are also one of the most versatile belts, as you can wear them just below the bust line, on the waist, on the hips, or through belt loops on pants or skirts.

The wide belt
This belt will add drama to almost any outfit. Opt for one that's as wide as your waist allows, and wear it over chunky knits or even over coats, as Kate does, to cinch in heavy fabrics and keep your silhouette feminine. A wide belt can accentuate your waist, enhance curves, and cleverly conceal any lumps and bumps.

The textured belt
Add contrast and interest to plain fabrics with a textured or shiny belt, such as Kate's mock-croc "Betony" seen here.

The statement color belt
To brighten up a Little Black Dress or to add subtle, elegant detail to colorful outfits, pick a belt in a bright color. The belt can either match or contrast other pieces in your outfit—it's up to you. Kate often pairs a chunky red belt from Reiss with a matching red coat.

The elastic belt
Worn on the waist, this tight-fitting belt will give you curves, even if you don't already have them (and helps control them if you do), creating a classic hourglass effect. For a different look, you can also wear an elastic belt lower down on your hips.

The Earrings Kate's earrings are very similar in design to her citrine and diamond Kiki McDonough earrings, which are thought to have been a Christmas present from William. Fashion observers suspect that the Duchess loved the first pair so much that she commissioned McDonough to create her an additional pair using different colored stones.

Kate's Custom LBD

The Dress Kate took the gold medal for style once more when she wore this beautiful dress to attend a reception for Great Britain's Olympic medalists, hosted by HM the Queen at Buckingham Palace on October 23, 2012. The champion athletes in attendance wore their official Olympic black suits adorned with their gold medals, and Kate carefully selected an outfit in a matching color palette.

The Duchess chose a black dress embellished with lace and gold flowers, designed by one of her go-to designers, Alice Temperley. The piece was made for the Duchess personally, frustrating fans who were knocked out by this twist on that favorite style stand-by: the Little Black Dress. Fashion writers thought the starting point for the dress was the "Esmeralda" from Temperley London's collection, as the lace detailing, belled sleeves, and ruffled hems were similar in style and shape to this off-the-rack piece. However, added to this simple base was gold, ivory, and dusky rose floral embroidery, sheer detailing over the décolletage, and a signature Kate staple: a belt in the form of a soft, satin bow.

Alice Temperley has spoken about how it feels to be a favorite designer of both Middleton sisters: "I'm flattered," she said. "They're the most humble, down-to-earth people I've ever dressed. They're completely easy and wonderful to work with, and they look great in the clothes. They know exactly what they like. When I was dressing them, I had no idea what a reaction the world would have," she added. "I hope that they always get the support that they deserve because they are truly good girls."

The Shoes On her feet, the Duchess wore her Jimmy Choo "Cosmic" pumps, which take the form of a classic heel but are stylistically notched up a level with the addition of a platform under the toes, giving the traditional look a more modern profile.

The Bracelet Kate wore her diamond flower cluster Art Deco bracelet to the royal reception. One of her favorite pieces of jewelry, it often graces her wrist on dressier occasions. It is thought to have been a gift from William, possibly once belonging to his mother, Princess Diana.

Customize like Kate

Kate's Temperley dress had embroidery and a fitted lace panel to make it unique for her. Even if you're not on a personal-name basis with designers, you, too, can create a one-of-a-kind piece with a little savvy sewing.

Embellish away
If you're skillful with a needle and thread, purchase some inexpensive sheer fabric and get creative. However, if you're less artistically inclined, most craft stores stock a selection of embroidered fabrics. Simply choose one you think will work and stitch the fabric panels onto sleeves and hemlines of a plain dress to add a touch of drama.

Belt up
With nothing more than a length of satin ribbon, you can add waist detailing (one of Kate's key fashion rules) to any outfit. Simply wrap a length of ribbon around your waistline and fasten with a neat bow.

Make a feature of modesty
By adding a sheer panel to the plunging neckline of her dress, Kate transformed this piece into a suitably demure dress for a Duchess attending a royal reception. You can do the same by simply purchasing a piece of sheer netting or lace in the same color as your dress and stitching it in place over the neckline and or arms.

Button up
An easy way to add a touch of your own personal style to a store-bought piece is to replace the buttons. Craft stores are full of interesting and unusual buttons, so look around for some truly unique options.

Add a dash of contrasting fabric
Update plain turtlenecks or cardigans by sewing a band of tweed or leather (perhaps salvaged from old unworn clothes) just above the bustline or onto the waist. You can also try sewing elbow patches to a sweater or blazer. This simple patch-up job adds instant designer detailing and flair to tired pieces.

FAR LEFT: Kate wore this striking cream chiffon Temperley dress, with black detailing at the cuffs, collar, and waist, for her first public appearance after her engagement announcement, when attending the Teenage Cancer Trust Christmas Spectacular in December 2010.

LEFT: The Duchess looks a true Queen of the South Pacific with her "crown" of flower garlands and the floral Alice by Temperley "Beatrice" dress she wore on the Polynesian island Tuvalu, during her South Pacific tour in September 2012.

RIGHT: While watching tennis at Wimbledon in June 2011, Kate stood out from the crowd in this on-theme white ruffled and pleated Temperley "Moriah" dress.

Kate's Sheer Beauty

The Dress Fashion and the University of St. Andrews have always played a big part in Kate's life. It was during a St. Andrews charity fashion event at a catwalk show in March 2002 that Kate first caught the eye of her fellow student, Prince William. After seeing his future wife modeling a mostly see-through dress (see page 22), the Prince apparently whispered to a friend: "Wow, Kate's hot!" This sheer dress, made from black and turquoise knitted silk by Charlotte Todd, fashion graduate of the University of the West of England, was sold at auction in 2011 for a staggering $125,000!

To show her support for her alma mater (and that of her patron husband, too), when the royal couple attended the 600th anniversary gala on November 8, 2012, Kate chose another sheer dress. . . although this time something much more sophisticated, from one of her favorite designers, Alice Temperley.

The show-stopping "Amoret" gown is made of luxurious French lace underlaid with a blush silk slip that accentuates the floral design. Typical Temperley detailing can also be found in the scalloping along the cuffs, hem, and the plunging neckline, a keyhole back, crepe bow belt, and a curved seam, which lends elegant movement to the skirt. The overall effect is a supremely feminine, timeless dress that is the ultimate in refined chic and evening glamour.

The gorgeous floor-length gown was, in fact, first seen on Kate at the premiere of Steven Spielberg's *War Horse* in January 2012 in London. However, this time the effect was slightly different. Never one to miss a fashion reference, Kate must have been aware that the sheer nature of this lace dress would recall the earlier, somewhat infamous, see-through dress of her student days. How typically clever of Kate to turn what is actually a demure dress into a rather racy inside fashion joke. Indeed, that fateful day was clearly on Kate's mind at the gala as she joked with a current female undergraduate at St. Andrews: "I hope you weren't involved in the fashion show—you never know what you are going to be asked to wear!"

The Shoes The Duchess also brought back her towering black suede Jimmy Choo "Cosmic" heels. The teetering platforms balanced the length of the gown and added extra height and drama to Kate's already statuesque frame.

RIGHT: Kate first debuted the "Amoret" gown at *War Horse* in January 2012, where she accessorized it with a black clutch.

The Brooch This gala event came just three days before the U.K.'s Remembrance Day on November 11, 2012—a period when many people wear a red poppy in memory of those who sacrificed their lives during active duty. A staunch supporter of the Armed Forces (with husband Prince William an active member of the Royal Air Force), Kate pinned a large poppy-shaped brooch, plated with 18-carat gold and inlaid with red and black crystals, to her dress. All profits raised from the sale of this Adrian Buckley-designed piece went to the Royal British Legion, a leading charity that supports serving and ex-Service personnel in the British Armed Forces. British designer Buckley founded his eponymous line in 1989 and has since won the prestigious award for Best Costume Jewellery four times at the U.K. Jewellery Awards.

The Bag Kate picked up on the poppy color in her ruby-red Alexander McQueen "Classic" clutch, albeit without the signature McQueen skull clasp. In its place at the center of the bowed bag was a custom clasp, embellished with three red rhinestones. This was another recycled piece—Kate having first carried it on the Thames Diamond Jubilee River Pageant, back in June 2012.

OPPOSITE: The simple Annoushka "Baroque Pearl Drop" earrings, top left, are one of Kate's favorites, as their classic, understated design works equally well with day and evening wear. Kate has been spotted wearing the beautiful diamond bracelet and matching diamond drop earrings, right and bottom right, which she paired with the gown at the *War Horse* premiere, to many formal evening functions. These were first seen on Kate's tour of Canada in 2011, but a designer has never been identified, and they are described only as being "a gift." This has led to speculation that they may have been a custom design, specially created as a present for her by Prince William.

Wear Sheer Fabrics with Class

Tracing Kate's love for sheer fabrics is a key way to see how her youthful experimentation has evolved into a mature style. Worn carefully, sheer fabric can be the epitome of sophistication and—unlike *that* runway dress—Kate has now mastered the art of demure when it comes to the transparent. Here are some of her style tricks:

Slip into something a little special
A nude slip will keep a sheer outfit classy, and also skim over any lumps and bumps—not that Kate has any to hide!

Play with patterns
Patterned sheer fabrics, such as lace, provide more coverage than the sheer netting in which young Kate once strutted down the catwalk.

Foxy folds
Another of Kate's style staples—the pleated skirt—works very well in sheer fabrics, such as chiffon, as the folds create layers, which prevent it from being too revealing.

Master the covered/uncovered look
A dress in a sheer fabric with long, bell-shaped sleeves and a full skirt is fast becoming a staple of Kate's wardrobe. The hint of flesh through the fabric adds glamour but the delicate sheer covering keeps things elegant.

Fabulous Retro Chic

The Dress Kate wore this exquisite emerald-green Mulberry dress to the opening of the "Treasures" exhibition at the Natural History Museum in London on November 27, 2012. The "Full Pleated Shirt Dress" from Mulberry's ready-to-wear collection features a Peter Pan collar, a plethora of pleats, a belted waist, and long balloon sleeves gathered at the cuff. The 100 percent silk dress has retro styling, including Mulberry's "Peace and Love" jacquard design, and the rich color is given the somewhat unglamorous official name of "cabbage!"

It is not the first time that Kate has been associated with classic British design house Mulberry. She took their "Polly Push" bag in midnight blue on her tour of Canada and has been spotted in a wool skirt by the brand while shopping in Chelsea. In fact, the exhibition was not the first time Kate has worn this particular piece. One year previously, almost to the day, she first wore what is, for the Duchess, an uncharacteristically "boho-styled" retro frock, while launching the Queen's Diamond Jubilee celebrations at Buckingham Palace.

Mulberry is well known for its quintessentially English style, so this more flamboyant dress was out of the ordinary not only for the Duchess, but also for the label itself. The company describes the dress as "prim and proper with a Mulberry twist. The full-pleated shirt dress will not let you blend into the crowd." Perhaps Kate felt safe experimenting with a brand like Mulberry, which has a solid reputation for classic style—here, she can play with a quirky look without fear of going too far.

The Shoes Kate once more stepped into her favorite Jimmy Choo "Cosmic" pumps—this time the matt suede fabric of the heels perfectly offset her shimmering silk dress.

The Hair Kate may have been wearing an old dress and shoes to a museum, but she did wear one brand new item that caused worldwide excitement: her hairstyle. Perhaps influenced by the boho dress, the Duchess chose a retro look that featured side bangs and flippy layers. The overall effect was not dissimilar to the famous style of 1970s star Farrah Fawcett—or indeed, as many observers were quick to point out—some of the hairstyles sported by Princess Diana in the early 1980s. Kate's new look is thought to have been created by her favorite hair salon—Richard Ward of Chelsea, London—and was widely deemed to be a great success, softening her face and adding sophistication.

Flip It like Kate

The Duchess's 1970s-inspired hairstyle is, in fact, pretty easy to achieve if you follow a few simple steps.

Embrace your dark side
Kate took her natural color up a shade from soft, light-tinged auburn tones to a sleeker, richer, chocolate-brown. Going for a slightly darker shade than your natural hair color will help create a fuller, sleeker look.

The benefits of bangs
Ask your hairdresser to cut the front section of your hair into long bangs at a steep angle because a straight, blunt cut can look too severe. Make sure it's left long enough to tuck behind the ears in case you have a change of heart!

Layer up
Ask your stylist for additional layers to be chopped into the lower lengths around your face to add texture, volume, and movement.

Big on body
When washing your hair, be sure to rinse out all traces of conditioner to prevent your hair from going limp. Then, while it's still wet, use a volumizing spray at the roots before you begin blow-drying.

Get to grips with your hair dryer
Towel dry your hair until it's about 90 percent dry, teasing it with your fingertips to encourage volume. Then, starting at the bottom, take 1–2 inch sections at a time, keeping the rest of your hair pinned out of the way. Wrap each section around a large, round, bristle brush, lift the hair up with maximum tension, and direct the dryer onto it for a few seconds. Use the cool setting on your dryer to fix each section before removing the brush, and then mist with a flexible light-hold hairspray.

Finally, get to work on your bangs
If your bangs have already dried, spritz them with a little cold water. Then, using a smaller, round brush, start drying with a rolling action. As the hair becomes drier, begin brushing the bangs at the desired angle to create a flip.

Finishing touches
In order for the curl to really last, put in some large Velcro curlers and leave for 10 minutes, blasting them with a hot hair dryer. Remove the rollers when your hair is cool, and use your fingertips to tease out the curls. Again, finish off with a spritz of hairspray.

Learn from the professionals
Kate's favorite Richard Ward salon is just one of many hairdressers that now offer master classes for the perfect blowout, so you can learn how to create a professional finish in the comfort of your own home.

LOOK 39

Tartan Celebration

The Coat Kate made a savvy style statement when she visited her old preparatory school, St. Andrew's in Pangbourne, Berkshire, on November 30, 2012. Her custom Alexander McQueen coat was made out of Black Watch tartan, which was both an appropriate choice for a visit that took place on St. Andrew's Day, and a clever reference to Kate's old school uniform. The three-check pattern featuring blue and green separated by black was very similar to the kilts worn by Kate as a pupil at the private school between 1986 and 1995. But the coat wasn't just an exercise in nostalgia—Kate was also picking up on a very current fashion trend, with tartan a key look on many Fall/Winter 2012 catwalks, including Chloé, Michael Kors, and Ralph Lauren, as well as McQueen.

For McQueen's Fall/Winter 2012 collections, Sarah Burton selected the very striking Black Watch tartan, belonging to Scotland's most famous elite army regiment, which dates back as far as 1729. At the time, the brand released the following statement about its fabric choice: "The use of the navy and dark-green plaid of Scotland's 3rd Battalion Regiment, the Black Watch, represents the brand's reverence for history and tradition."

Kate's coatdress was, in fact, custom-made, but it incorporates some elements of the Alexander McQueen "Black Watch" coat, from the label's hipper and more affordable diffusion line, McQ. Both the full skirt and oversized flaps at the hips reflect the original design. However, Kate's coat was cut from a lighter weight of the fabric, making it a little easier to wear.

The Boots Once again, Kate donned her favorite black Aquatalia "Rhumba" boots, pulling them over thick black pantyhose. And, once again, the versatile and practical boots didn't let her down on the athletic field. Seemingly delighted to be back on familiar turf, the former team captain showed off her skills on the school's new hockey field, looking totally at ease—even in high heels!

The Earrings Kate picked out the navy in her coatdress in her dazzling sapphire and diamond earrings. This reworked pair of her late mother-in-law Diana's earrings is clearly a favorite with the Duchess, as she has worn them on many occasions (see also Look 6, page 42). The heirloom jewelry also helped underline the shades of Diana that many observers saw in her still-new, side-swept hairstyle.

Tartan It Up

The Duchess of Cambridge has a fondness for this traditional checkered fabric, and twice carried a folded Strathearn tartan scarf in a nod to her Scottish title, the Countess of Strathearn. The first time she sported the scarf was with her scarlet Alexander McQueen outfit for the Thames Diamond Jubilee Pageant in London on June 2012 (see Look 22, page 96) and then again in July in Edinburgh, when she watched Prince William honored with the highest possible title in Scotland: the Knight of the Thistle.

On this occasion, Kate's tartan coat may have matched the student uniforms of her old prep school, but there was nothing schoolgirl about this sophisticated outfit. Here are some dos and don'ts for wearing this traditional Scottish fabric in a stylish, grown-up way:

Do remember it's a winter fabric
Tartan is too heavy for summer but you can still keep the thick fabric looking feminine by choosing pieces in well-tailored shapes.

Don't overdo it
One piece of tartan is always enough, as Kate knows well. Wear tartan alone as the main feature item in any outfit, as the pattern looks stunning in a solid block, but the effect will be lost when worn on top of matching tartan accessories. Similarly, a touch of tartan—in the form of a scarf or purse—adds another dimension to an otherwise plain outfit.

Do wear it for all occasions
Tartan is a versatile fabric that can be dressed up or down. Add simple black accessories and heels for formal events, or combine with denim and long boots for more casual daywear.

Don't forget tartan was originally worn by men
To soften its masculine look, try choosing feminine shapes such as Kate's full-skirted "fit and flare" coat.

Do choose the size of your tartan plaid with care
This is not the kind of fabric where bigger is better for most women—both petite and larger frames will find finer checks more flattering than bold, large designs.

OPPOSITE: Despite Kate's fresh-faced appearance, just three days after she wore this stylish tartan ensemble to visit her old school, it was announced that the Duchess was pregnant and had been suffering from a severe form of morning sickness. This led to Kate spending a few days in the hospital, but Buckingham Palace soon assured the nation that Kate and the baby, due in July 2013, were in good health.

Kate's Blooming

The Dress When the Duchess of Cambridge attended the unveiling of her portrait at the National Portrait Gallery in London on January 12, 2013, she was glowing with health, and her slender frame hinted at the first signs of a still-tiny baby bump. The mother-to-be displayed a rosy complexion with pink cheeks, and despite looking her usual slim self, she did appear a little fuller in the face. One thing seemed clear— the Duchess appeared to be back on form following her brief hospitalization with severe morning sickness.

Despite the media distraction caused by her pregnancy, Kate's impeccable sense of style shone through as she donned this elegant burgundy chiffon dress for an event that would inevitably put her under the spotlight. The "Sofie Rae" dress was from her chain store favorite, Whistles, and was actually part of their Autumn/Winter 2011 collection. The seasonal design is 100 percent silk, with long, floaty sleeves, a deep V-neckline, and open-neck with collarless trim. Its full, pleated skirt falls flatteringly to just-below-knee length and gathers at the waist for definition. Kate chose to add her own plain wide ribbon-style black belt to pull the look together, matching with her black shoes and clutch purse.

Not yet ready for maternity-wear and always wanting to get maximum use out of a purchase, the Duchess was previously spotted wearing this dress when she and Prince William traveled to Denmark back in November 2011 for the charity UNICEF, and she also wore it under a plum wool coat by an independent British designer, when she visited Newcastle in October 2012.

While Kate's fashion sense was typically faultless, the official portrait of her, by British-born artist Paul Emsley, inspired more mixed reviews, as many commentators thought the likeness unflattering. Some critics thought the painting made the Duchess look old, while U.K. newspaper the *Daily Mail* reported that the portrait had been called "rotten." The Duchess herself, however, said she was thrilled with the results, and husband Prince William also had high praise for the painting, stating: "It's beautiful, it's absolutely beautiful." To pose for the portrait, Kate wore a navy sleeveless, silk blouse by French Connection called the "Sub Silky Tie Top," and accessorized it with the sapphire and diamond earrings that were made from a set belonging to Princess Diana.

The Necklace To complement the "Sofie Rae" dress, Kate chose to wear her much-loved Asprey 167 Button Pendant, which nestled perfectly in the dress's deep V-neck. The necklace features white pavé diamonds surrounding a central amethyst, all set in 18-carat white gold. Demand for the item since Kate was first seen wearing it in 2011 was so high that jewelers Asprey re-issued the previously discontinued piece in September 2012. Asprey is one of the U.K.'s oldest fine jewelers, dating back to 1781, with a flagship store on London's New Bond Street. Asprey has a long association with royalty, supplying crowns, coronets, and scepters for royal families around the world, and currently holds a Royal Warrant of appointment from the Prince of Wales.

The Shoes The early stages of pregnancy didn't seem to affect Kate's penchant for high heels, and here she wears another previously seen pair, her Episode "Angel" shoes in black suede. The Episode brand is sold only in U.K. department store House of Fraser. Kate was first spotted wearing these heels during the Diamond Jubilee visit to Leicester in March 2012.

How to Dress your Bump

Kate's pregnancy style remains unchanged—chic, elegant, ladylike shapes and a seamless blend of chain store and designer labels. Many first-time mothers-to-be make the mistake of not wearing their favorite clothes early in their pregnancy, but Kate understands that just because you have a bump to dress, it doesn't mean you have to lose your sense of style. Here's how to look good in clothes that have room for a baby bump, but still show off your figure and style credentials:

Be beautifully wrapped
Wrap dresses and tops make a great choice for moms-to-be, as the V-neck front flatters the chest, while the tied waist allows for the growth of the bump. Wraps work for both day and evening, and the springy jersey fabric allows you to get away with your normal size for the first six months of pregnancy.

Be biased
Kate loves dresses and skirts that are cut to accentuate curves, and the soft-draping, curve-accentuating lines are perfect for pregnancy, as they have more "give" than straight-cut ones, and will sit well on your bump as it gets bigger.

Find full-term friends in your closet
There will probably be a few things in your closet that you can wear throughout your pregnancy with a little bit of alteration. For example, cardigans and shirts can work when left open with a long camisole top underneath.

Say no to frills
As you will be carrying plenty of bulk on your top half, don't add to it with overly frilly tops. Keep detail to a minimum.

Show off your shape
Define your figure by choosing long tops with ties that fasten under the bust or at the side. For more glamorous evening events, add thick ribbon or belts to shapeless tops and dresses.

Royal Maternity Wear

Thankfully Kate has a lot of options when it comes to maternity wear, because stores and fashion designers have finally realized that women want to remain looking chic during their pregnancy—they don't want to hide their bumps in shapeless smocks for nine months. Here are some of the best places to shop for Kate-style maternity fashion:

ASOS Maternity Collection, *www.asos.com*
Rumor has it that Kate stocked up on some pretty items from the online store's maternity line, which features fashion-forward dresses, jeans, and lingerie.

Gap, *www.gap.com*
In January 2013, Kate was spotted browsing the Chelsea, London, branch of Gap, everybody's favorite go-to for comfy, well-cut casuals. And no wonder—they have a fantastic line of maternity jeans, which have the same cut as their standard denims, but with an added elastic extending waistline that grows with your bump.

Isabella Oliver, *www.isabellaoliver.com*
This classy online store has become the savior of many style-conscious moms-to-be who love their flattering runched jersey tops and fabulous collection of wrap dresses, which promise to add glamour to any bump.

Séraphine, *www.seraphine.com*
A great choice for chic maternity clothes that flaunt, rather than hide, your curves, Séraphine would be perfect for Kate as many of their colors and shapes closely echo Kate's signature style: like their purple knot dress (top left), stone wool coat (bottom left), and gray chiffon and sequin dress (opposite).

Top Shop Maternity, *www.topshop.com*
The Duchess has always been a fan of this store's affordable but on-trend offerings, so it makes perfect sense for her to choose from their great collection of trendy mom-to-be essential wear.

Kate's Style Directory

Want to know where Kate buys her jeans or where to find her go-to shops and labels for formal and casual wear? Our handy and extensive directory lists the key stores and where to locate them.

As with the 40 classic looks on the previous pages, one of the attributes that propels Kate from simply stylish into style icon territory is her ability to put together a complete ensemble. Not only does she choose beautiful dresses, elegant coats, and chic separates, but she also pays careful attention to every last detail and knows how to pick the perfect accessory. Whether it is choosing the ideal Kiki McDonough topaz earrings to finish off a look, the perfect L.K. Bennett clutch bag, or some on-theme R. Soles cowboy boots, Kate has the eye of a professional stylist. Here we list her beloved accessories brands as well as her all-time chain store favorites, such as Reiss and Zara, plus a few of her lesser-known haunts, including the British brands Episode at House of Fraser and Russell & Bromley.

The list, of course, wouldn't be Kate's unless it included her designer labels of choice, such as Alexander McQueen, Alice Temperley, Emilia Wickstead, and Issa. And for those finishing touches, we detail where to get your hands on items from her makeup brands to her perfume of choice.

Accessories

Aquatalia by Marvin K
U.S.A.
Neiman Marcus
Maple & Paulding Avenue
White Plains
New York NY 10601
1-914-428-2000
www.neimanmarcus.com

Saks Fifth Avenue
611 5th Avenue
New York NY 10022
1-877-551-7257
www.saksfifthavenue.com

Canada
Available at many independent
retailers throughout the country,
including the following:

Brown's Shoes
3035 Boul. Carrefour Laval
Laval, QC H7T 1C7
1-450-681-4924
www.brownsshoes.com

Brown's Shoes
1 Promenade Circle
Thornhill ON L4J 4P8
1-905-764-1444
www.brownsshoes.com

Brown's Shoes
300 Borough Drive
Scarborough ON M1P 4P5
1-416-290-5158
www.brownsshoes.com

Davids
Markio Designs Inc.
1200 Bay Street
Toronto ON M5R 2A5
1-416-929-9629
www.davidsfootwear.com

Holt Renfrew
2452 Laurier Boulevard
Quebec City QC G1V 2L1
1-418-656-6783
www.holtrenfrew.com

Holt Renfrew
737 Dunsmuir Street
Vancouver BC V7Y 1E4
1-604-681-3121
www.holtrenfrew.com

Jean-Paul Fortin
2050 De Celles
Quebec G2C 1X8
1-418-845-5369
www.jeanpaulfortin.com

Ogilvy
1307 Sainte-Catherine Street W.
Montreal QC H3G 1P7
1-514-842-7711
www.ogilvycanada.com

U.K.
Russell & Bromley
24–25 New Bond Street
London W1S 2PS
+44 (0) 20 7629 6903
www.russellandbromley.co.uk

Australia
Stuart Weitzman for Hermanns
175 Collins Street
Melbourne VIC 3000
03-9522-9709
*www.hermanns.com.au/
Hermanns.asp*

Le Chameau
U.K.
Bestboots Ltd
Coates Farm
Nettleton
Wiltshire SN14 7NS
+44 (0) 1249 783530
www.bestboots.co.uk

Cedarstone Limited
Callimore Farm
Droitwich
Worcestershire WR9 0NS
+44 (0) 1299 851767
www.le-chameau-clothing.co.uk

John Norris of Penrith
21 Victoria Road
Penrith
Cumbria CA11 8HP
+44 (0) 1768 864211
www.johnnorris.co.uk

Out of the City Ltd
Ordnance Road
Buckshaw Village
Chorley
Lancashire PR7 7EL
+44 (0) 1772 977321
www.outofthecity.co.uk

Philip Morris & Son
21 Widemarsh Street
Hereford HR4 9EE
+44 (0) 1432 377089
www.philipmorrisdirect.co.uk

Jimmy Choo
U.S.A.
240 North Rodeo Drive
Beverly Hills
Los Angeles CA 90210
1-310-860-9045
www.jimmychoo.com

Bloomingdale's
845 Market Street
San Francisco CA 94103
1-415-856-5431
www.jimmychoo.com

716 Madison Avenue
New York NY 10065
1-212-759-7078
www.jimmychoo.com

U.K.
32 Sloane Street
London SW1X 9NR
+44 (0) 20 7823 1051
www.jimmychoo.com

27 New Bond Street
London W1S 2RH
+44 (0) 20 7493 5858
www.jimmychoo.com

Australia
Chadstone Shopping Centre
1341 Dandenong Road
Chadstone VIC 3148
61-0-39038-10-84
www.jimmychoo.com

MLC Centre
41 Castlereagh Street
Sydney NSW 2000
61-2-8666-06-06
www.jimmychoo.com

Westfield Bondi Junction
500 Oxford Street
Bondi Junction NSW 2022
61-2-9078-86-68
www.jimmychoo.com

Jane Corbett
U.K.
Roxtons
10/11 Bridge Street
Hungerford
Berkshire RG17 OEH
+44 (0) 7557 868260
www.janecorbett.co.uk
(Studio visits by appointment only)

Episode
U.K.
House of Fraser
318 Oxford Street
London W1C 1HF
+44 (0) 1236 634 567
www.houseoffraser.co.uk

Salvatore Ferragamo
U.S.A.
655 5th Ave
New York NY 10022
1-212-759-3822
www.ferragamo.com

45 North Michigan Avenue
Chicago IL 60611
1-312-397-0464
www.ferragamo.com

8500 Beverly Boulevard No. 770
Los Angeles CA 90048
1-310-652-0279
www.ferragamo.com

100 Huntington Avenue
Boston MA 02116
1-617-859-4924
www.ferragamo.com

U.K.
24 Old Bond Street
London W1S 4AL
+44 (0) 20 7629 5007
www.ferragamo.com

207 Sloane Street
London SW1X 9QX
+44 (0) 20 7838 7730
www.ferragamo.com

Westfield
London W12 7SL
+44 (0) 20 8743 0212
www.ferragamo.com

Harrods
87–135 Brompton Road
London SW1X 0NA
+44 (0) 20 7730 1234
www.ferragamo.com

Mitsukoshi
14–20 Lower Regent Street
London SW1Y 4PH
+44 (0) 20 7839 6714
www.ferragamo.com

Selfridges
400 Oxford Street
London W1A 1AB
+44 (0) 20 7318 2326
www.ferragamo.com

Australia
David Jones
100 Rundle Mall
Adelaide SA 5000
61-8-8305-3269
www.ferragamo.com

45 Collins Street
Melbourne VIC 3000
61-3-9654-5066
www.ferragamo.com

45 Castlereagh Street
Sydney NSW 2000
61-2-9221-3036
www.ferragamo.com

Sylvia Fletcher for James Lock
U.K.
Lock & Co. Hatters
6 St James's Street
London SW1A 1EF
+44 (0) 20 7930 8874
www.lockhatters.co.uk

French Sole Ltd
U.K.
26 Brook Street
London W1K 5DQ
+44 (0) 20 7493 2678
www.frenchsole.com

6 Ellis Street
London SW1X 9AL
+44 (0) 20 7730 3771
www.frenchsole.com

323 King's Road
London SW3 5EP
+44 (0) 20 7351 1634
www.frenchsole.com

61 Marylebone Lane
London W1U 2PA
+44 (0) 20 7486 0021
www.frenchsole.com

Givenchy Sunglasses
U.S.A.
Barneys New York
660 Madison Avenue
New York NY 10021
1-212-826-8900
www.givenchy.com

Bergdorf Goodman
754 5th Avenue
New York NY 10019
1-212-753-7300
www.givenchy.com

Jeffrey
449 West 14th Street
New York NY 10014
1-212-206-1272
www.givenchy.com

Canada
Holt Renfrew
50 Bloor Street
Toronto M4W 1A1
1-416-922-2333
www.givenchy.com

La Maison Simon
977 Sainte-Catherine Ouest
Montreal QC H3B 4W3
1-514-282-1840
www.givenchy.com

SSense
9600 Meilleur
Montreal QC H2N 2ES
1-514-384-1906
www.givenchy.com

U.K.
Dover Street Market
17–18 Dover Street
London W1S 4LT
+44 (0) 20 7518 0680
www.givenchy.com

Harrods
87–135 Brompton Road
London SW1X 7XL
+44 (0) 20 7730 1234
www.givenchy.com

Harvey Nichols
109–125 Knightsbridge
London SW1X 7RJ
+44 (0) 20 7235 5000
www.givenchy.com

Anya Hindmarch
U.S.A.
29 East 60th Street
New York NY 10022
1-212-750-3974
www.anyahindmarch.com

118 South Robertson Boulevard
Los Angeles CA 90048
1-310-271-9707
www.anyahindmarch.com

U.K.
15–17 Pont Street
London SW1X 9EH
+44 (0) 20 7838 9177
www.anyahindmarch.com

63 Ledbury Road
London W11 2AJ
+44 (0) 20 7792 4427
www.anyahindmarch.com

118 New Bond Street
London W1S 1EW
+44 (0) 20 7493 1628
www.anyahindmarch.com

157–158 Sloane Street
London SW1X 9AB
+44 (0) 20 7730 0961
www.anyahindmarch.com

Jaeger
U.K.
200–206 Regent Street
London W1R 6BN
+44 (0) 20 7979 1100
www.jaeger.co.uk

102 George Street
Edinburgh EH2 3DF
+44 (0) 131 225 8811
www.jaeger.co.uk

20 Milsom Street
Bath
Avon BA1 1DE
+44 (0) 1225 466415
www.jaeger.co.uk

Kiki McDonough
U.K.
12 Symons Street
London SW3 2TJ
+44 (0) 20 7730 3323
www.kiki.co.uk

Also available through Astley
Clarke: *www.astleyclarke.com*

L.K. Bennett
U.S.A.
Bloomingdale's
59th Street & Lexington Avenue
New York NY 10022
1-212-705-2000
www.lkbennett.com

900 North Michigan Avenue
Chicago IL 60611
1-312-374-0958
www.lkbennett.com

Houston Galleria
5085 Westheimer Road
Houston TX 77056
1-713-961-0009
www.lkbennett.com

U.K.
164–166 King's Road
London SW3 4UR
+44 (0) 20 7351 9659
www.lkbennett.com

94 Marylebone High Street
London W1U 4RY
+44 (0) 20 7224 0319
www.lkbennett.com

45–45a George Street
Edinburgh EH2 2HT
+44 (0) 131 226 3370
www.lkbennett.com

Victoria Square
Belfast BT1 4QG
+44 (0) 2890 238 292
www.lkbennett.com

St Davids Two
Tregegar Street
Cardiff CF10 2FB
+44 (0) 29 2034 1143
www.lkbennett.com

Pied à Terre
U.K.
House of Fraser
318 Oxford Street
London W1C 1HF
+44 (0) 1236 634567
www.houseoffraser.co.uk

Prada
U.S.A.
312 South Galena Street
Aspen CO 81611
1-970-925-7001
www.prada.com

8500 Beverly Boulevard
Space 739
Beverly Hills CA 90048
1-310-228-1400
www.prada.com

3200 Las Vegas Boulevard South
Las Vegas NV 89109
1-702-699-7106
www.prada.com

Canada
Holt Renfrew
510 8th Avenue SW
Calgary AB T2P 4HG
1-403-269-7341
www.prada.com

Holt Renfrew
737 Dunsmuir Street
Vancouver V7Y E4
1-604-681-3121
www.prada.com

U.K.
16–18 Old Bond Street
London W1S 4PS
+44 (0) 20 7647 5000
www.prada.com

House of Fraser
11–45 Buchanan Street
Glasgow G1 3HL
+44 (0) 141 221 3880
www.prada.com

Selfridges & Co.
1 Exchange Square
Manchester M31BD
+44 (0) 161 838 0710
www.prada.com

Australia
David Jones
86–108 Castlereagh Street
Sydney NSW 2000
61-2-9266-5249
www.prada.com

Shop 1, The Moroccan
11 Elkhorn Avenue
Surfers Paradise QLD 4217
61-7-5539-8858
www.prada.com

75–77 Collins Street
Melbourne VIC 3000
61-03-96630978
www.prada.com

R. Soles
U.K.
109A King's Road
London SW3 4PA
+44 (0) 20 7351 5520
www.rsoles.com

Rupert Sanderson
U.K.
19 Bruton Place
London W1J 6LZ
+44 (0) 20 7491 2260
www.rupertsanderson.com

2a Hans Road
London SW3 1RX
+44 (0) 20 7584 9249
www.rupertsanderson.com

Emmy Scarterfield
U.K.
Emmy Shoes
65 Cross Street
London N1 2BB
+44 (0) 20 7704 0012
www.emmyshoes.co.uk

Smithbilt Hats (Stetsons)
Canada
1103 12th Street Southeast
Calgary AB T2G 3H7
1-403-244-9131
www.smithbilthats.com

Jane Taylor Millinery
U.K.
3 Filmer Mews
75 Filmer Road
London SW6 7JF
+44 (0) 20 8393 2333
www.janetaylormillinery.com

Stuart Weitzman
Canada
3035 Boulevard le Carrefour
Laval QC H7T 1C8
1-450-973-1468
http://uk.stuartweitzman.com

Chinook Center
6455 Macleod Trail SW
Calgary AB T2H 0K9
1-403-265-0551
http://uk.stuartweitzman.com

2305 Rockland
Mont-Royal QC H3P 3E9
1-514-735-6344
http://uk.stuartweitzman.com

Wilbur & Gussie
U.S.A.
Gywnn's of Mount Pleasant
916 Houston Northcutt Blvd
Mt. Pleasant SC 29464
1-843-884-9518
www.wilburandgussie.com

Mildred Hoit
265 Sunrise Avenue
Palm Beach FL 334 80
1-561-833-6010
www.wilburandgussie.com

Vivi Shoes
503 West Lancaster Avenue
Wayne PA 19087
1-610-688-6732
www.wilburandgussie.com

U.K. and Ireland
Fenwick
63 New Bond Street
London W1S 1RJ
+44 (0) 20 7629 9161
www.wilburandgussie.com

Liberty
Regent Street
London W1B 5AH
+44 (0) 20 7734 1234
www.wilburandgussie.com

Harvey Nichols Dublin
Dundrum Town Centre
Dublin 16
+353 (0) 1291 0488
www.wilburandgussie.com

*Chain
Store &
Designer*

Alexander McQueen
U.S.A.
417 West 14th Street
New York NY 10014
1-212-645-1797
www.alexandermcqueen.com

8379 Melrose Ave
Los Angeles CA 90069
1-323-782-4983
www.alexandermcqueen.com

Bal Harbour
9700 Collins Avenue
Miami FLA 33154
1-305-866-2839
www.alexandermcqueen.com

U.K.
4–5 Old Bond Street
London W1S 4PD
+44 (0) 20 7355 0088
www.alexandermcqueen.com

Amanda Wakeley
U.K.
175–177 Fulham Road
London SW3 6JW
+44 (0) 20 7352 7143
www.amandawakeley.com

Harvey Nichols
109–125 Knightsbridge
London SW1X 7RJ
+44 (0) 20 7235 5000
www.amandawakeley.com

Harvey Nichols
107–111 Briggate Street
Leeds LS1 6AZ
+44 (0) 113 245 8119
www.amandawakeley.com

Harvey Nichols
30–34 St Andrews Square
Edinburgh EH2 3AD
+44 (0) 131 524 8388
www.amandawakeley.com

Harvey Nichols
21 New Cathedral Street
Manchester M3 1RE
+44 (0) 161 828 8864
www.amandawakeley.com

Banana Republic
U.S.A.
552 Broadway
New York NY 10012
1-212-334-2109
www.bananarepublic.gap.com

San Francisco Centre
865 Market Street
San Francisco CA 94103
1-415-546-0340
www.bananarepublic.gap.com

Beverly Center
8500 Beverly Blvd
Los Angeles CA 90048
1-310-652-0759
www.bananarepublic.gap.com

Marketplace Cntr-MA
200 State Street
Boston MA 02109
1-617-439-0016
www.bananarepublic.gap.com

U.K.
224 Regent Street
London W1B 3BR
020 7758 3550
www.bananarepublic.co.uk

23 King's Road
Duke of York Square
London SW3 4LY
+44 (0) 20 7730 4704
www.bananarepublic.co.uk

The Trafford Centre
Manchester M17 8BN
+44 (0) 161 748 4613
www.bananarepublic.co.uk

Beulah London
U.S.A.
No stores but will ship abroad.
www.beulahlondon.com

U.K.
14 Grosvenor Crescent
London SW1X 7EE
+44 (0) 20 7235 3818
www.beulahlondon.com

Harvey Nichols
109–125 Knightsbridge
London SW1X 7RJ
+44 (0) 20 7235 5000
www.beulahlondon.com

Kim Vine
84 The High Street
Marlborough
Wiltshire SN8 1HF
+44 (0) 1672 519937
www.beulahlondon.com

Christopher Kane
U.S.A.
Barneys
3325 Las Vegas Boulevard South
Las Vegas NV 89109
1-702-629-4200
www.barneys.com

U.K.
Browns
6c Sloane Street
London SW1X 9LE
+44 (0) 20 7514 0040
www.brownsfashion.com

Question Air
129 Church Road
London SW13 9HR
+44 (0) 20 8741 0816
www.question-air.com

Emilia Wickstead
U.K.
28 Cadogan Place
London SW1X 9RX
+44 (0) 20 7235 1104
www.emiliawickstead.com

Erdem
U.S.A.
Barney's New York
9570 Wilshire Blvd.
Beverly Hills CA 90212
1-310-276-4400
www.erdem.co.uk

Saks Fifth Avenue
384 Post Street
San Francisco CA 94108
1-415-086-4300
www.erdem.co.uk

Canada
Holt Renfrew
1300 Rue Sherbrooke Ouest
Montreal QC H3G 1H9
1-514-842-5111
www.erdem.co.uk

50 Bloor Street W
Toronto ON M4W 3L8
1-416-922-2333
www.erdem.co.uk

U.K. and Ireland
Selfridges
400 Oxford Street
London W1A 1AB
+44 (0) 20 7318 2326
www.erdem.co.uk

Thomas Brown
88–95 Grafton Street
Dublin 2
+353 (0) 1605 6666
www.erdem.co.uk

Goldsign
U.K.
Selfridges
400 Oxford Street
London W1A 1AB
+44 (0) 20 7318 2326
www.gold-sign-jeans.com

Hobbs
U.K.
37 Brompton Road
London SW3 1DE
+44 (0) 20 7225 2137
www.hobbs.co.uk

115 High Street
Oxford OX1 4BX
+44 (0) 1865 249 437
www.hobbs.co.uk

37 George Street
Richmond
London TW9 1HY
+44 (0) 20 8948 6720
www.hobbs.co.uk

Hudson
U.K.
Mee
9a Bartlett Street
Bath BA1 2QZ
+44 (0) 1225 442250
www.hudsonjeans.com

Mottoo
12 Duke Street
Brighton BN1 1AH
+44 (0) 1273 326 633
www.hudsonjeans.com

Trilogy
63 Weymouth Street
London W1G 8NU
+44 (0) 20 7486 8085
www.hudsonjeans.com

Australia
Mrs Watson
155 Sailors Bay Road
Northbridge NSW 2063
612-9958-1516
www.hudsonjeans.com

Momento
4 Manuka Circle
Manuka
Canberra ACT 2603
612-6295-1146
www.hudsonjeans.com

Page One
273 George Street
Sydney City NSW 2000
612-9252-6895
www.hudsonjeans.com

Issa
U.S.A.
Net-A-Porter
www.net-a-porter.com

U.K.
12 Lots Road
London SW10 0QD
+44 (0) 20 7352 4241
www.issalondon.com

89 Eastbourne Mews
London W2 6LQ
+44 (0) 20 7262 3124
www.issalondon.com

Harrods
87–135 Brompton Road
London SW1X 7XL
+44 (0) 20 7730 1234
www.issalondon.com

J Brand
U.S.A.
Suite 1D
811 Traction Ave
Los Angeles CA 90013
1-213-620-9797
www.jbrandjeans.com

40 Grants Ave
San Francisco CA 94108
1-415-982-5726
www.jbrandjeans.com

Canada
Aritzia
6551 No. 3 Road
Richmond BC V6Y 2B6
1-604-244-1614
www.jbrandjeans.com

Aritzia
701 West George Street
Vancouver BC V7Y 1AL
1-604-681-9301
www.jbrandjeans.com

U.K.
House of Fraser
Stores throughout the U.K.,
including:
318 Oxford Street
London W1C 1HF
+44 (0) 1236 634567
www.houseoffraser.co.uk

Australia
Debs
24 Ocean Beach Road
Sorrento VIC 3943
03-5984-1617
www.jbrandjeans.com

Mazal
Shop 2002
Westfield Sydney City
Sydney NSW 2022
61-404-875-111
www.jbrandjeans.com

Jenny Packham
U.S.A.
Gabriella New York
400 W 14th Street
New York NY 10014
1-212-206-1915
www.jennypackham.com

U.K.
3a Carlos Place (ready-to-wear)
Mount Street
London W1K 3AN
+44 (0) 20 7493 6295
www.jennypackham.com

75 Elizabeth Street (bridal, by
appointment only)
London SW1W 9PJ
+44 (0) 20 7730 2264
www.jennypackham.com

34 Elizabeth Street (accessories)
London SW1W 9NZ
+44 (0) 20 7730 4883
www.jennypackham.com

Katherine Hooker
U.K.
19 Ashburnham Road
London SW10 0PG
+44 (0) 20 7352 5091
www.katherinehooker.com

Libélula
U.K.
Austique
330 King's Road
London SW3 5UR
+44 (0) 20 7376 3663
www.libelula-studio.com

Austique
40 New Cavendish Street
London W1G 8UD
+44 (0) 20 7487 3468
www.libelula-studio.com

Katherine Bird
20 Battersea Rise
London SW11 1EE
+44 (0) 20 7228 2235
www.libelula-studio.com

Katie and Jo
253 New King's Road
London SW6 4RB
+44 (0) 20 7736 5304
www.libelula-studio.com

L.K. Bennett
(see Accessories, page 165)

M by Missoni
U.S.A.
Neiman Marcus
737 North Michigan Avenue
Chicago IL 60611
1-31-2642 5900
www.m-missoni.com

Saks Fifth Avenue
9634 Wilshire Boulevard
Beverly Hills CA 90212
1-310-275-4211
www.m-missoni.com

Canada
Holt Renfrew
25 The West Mallon
Toronto M9C 1B8
1-416-621-9900
www.m-missoni.com

U.K.
Harrods
87–135 Brompton Road
London SW1X 7XL
+44 (0) 20 7730 1234
www.m-missoni.com

Harvey Nichols
109–125 Knightsbridge
London SW1X 7RJ
+44 (0) 20 7235 5000
www.m-missoni.com

Australia
Cyberia
579 Chapel Street
South Yarra
Melbourne VIC 41059
61-3-9824-1339
www.m-missoni.com

Spence & Lyda
Surry Hills
Sydney NSW 2010
61-2-921-26747
www.m-missoni.com

Matthew Williamson
U.S.A.
415 West 14th Street
New York NY 10014
1-212-255-9881
www.matthewwilliamson.com

U.K.
28 Bruton Street
London W1J 6QH
+44 (0) 20 7629 6200
www.matthewwilliamson.com

Mulberry
U.S.A.
Tysons Galleria
2001 International Drive
Mclean VA 22102
1-888-685-6856
www.mulberry.com

166 Grant Avenue
San Francisco CA 94108
1-888-685-6856
www.mulberry.com

U.K.
26 Multrees Walk
Edinburgh EH1 3DQ
+44 (0) 131 557 5439
www.mulberry.com

House of Fraser
32–48 Promenade
Cheltenham GL50 1HP
+44 (0) 1242 521300
www.mulberry.com

Australia
Westfield Shopping Centre
188 Pitt Street
Sydney NSW 2000
61-28246-9160
www.mulberry.com

Penelope Chilvers
U.S.A.
Erica Wilson
25–27 Main Street
Nantucket MA 02554
1-508-228-988
www.penelopechilvers.com

The Gallerie
520 E Durant Ave 102
Aspen CO 81611
1-970-544-4893
www.penelopechilvers.com

U.K.
The Cross
141 Portland Road
London W11 4LR
+44 (0) 20 7727 6760
www.penelopechilvers.com

Lynx
20 West Park
Harrogate
North Yorkshire HG1 1BJ
01423 523845
www.penelopechilvers.com

Project D
U.K.
Austique Chelsea
330 King's Road
London SW3 5UR
+44 (0) 20 7376 4555
www.projectdlondon.com

Matches
13 Hill Street
Richmond
London TW9 1SX
+44 (0) 20 8332 9733
www.projectdlondon.com

Square
15 Old Bond Street
Bath BA1 1BP
+44 (0) 1225 464 997
www.projectdlondon.com

Australia
David Jones
86–108 Castlereagh Street
Sydney NSW 2000
02-9266-5544
www.davidjones.com.au

Emilio Pucci
U.S.A.
Crystals at City Centre
3720 Las Vegas Boulevard South
Las Vegas NV 89158
1-702-262-9671
http://home.emiliopucci.com

Saks Fifth Avenue
611 5th Avenue
New York NY 10022
1-212-753-4000
http://home.emiliopucci.com

U.K.
170 Sloane Street
London SW1X 9QG
+44 (0) 20 7201 8171
http://home.emiliopucci.com

Harrods
87–135 Brompton Road
London SW1X 0NA
+44 (0) 20 7730 1234
http://home.emiliopucci.com

Selfridges
400 Oxford Street
London W1A 1AB
+44 (0) 20 7318 3369
http://home.emiliopucci.com

Ralph Lauren
U.S.A.
109 Prince Street
New York NY 10012
1-212-625-1660
www.ralphlauren.com

2040 Fillmore Street
San Francisco CA 94115
1-415-440-6536
www.ralphlauren.com

U.K.
1 New Bond Street
London W1S 3RL
+44 (0) 20 7535 4600
www.ralphlauren.co.uk

105–109 Fulham Road
London SW3 6RL
+44 (0) 20 7590 7990
www.ralphlauren.co.uk

233–235 Westbourne Grove
London W11 2SE
+44 (0) 20 7313 7590
www.ralphlauren.co.uk

Australia
David Jones
80–108 Castlereagh Street
Sydney NSW 2000
01-02-9266-5581
www.ralphlauren.com

Reiss
U.S.A.
900 North Michigan Avenue
Chicago IL 60611
1-312-440-4460
www.reiss.com

Beverly Center
Bloomingdale's
8500 Beverly Boulevard
Los Angeles CA 90048
1-310-360-2700
www.reiss.com

309–313 Bleecker Street
New York NY 10014
1-212-488-2411
www.reiss.com

U.K.
26 Trinity Street
Cambridge CB2 1TB
+44 (0) 1223 308 733
www.reiss.com

114 King's Road
London SW3 4TX
+44 (0) 20 7589 0439
www.reiss.com

10 Hampstead High Street
London NW3 1PX
+44 (0) 20 7435 1542
www.reiss.com

Roksanda Ilincic
U.S.A.
Elizabeth Charles
2056 Fillmore Street
San Francisco CA 94115
1-415-440-2100
www.roksandailincic.com

Kirna Zabete
96 Greene Street
New York NY 10012
1-212-941-9656
www.roksandailincic.com

Opening Ceremony
451 North La Cienega Boulevard
Los Angeles CA 90048
1-310-652-1120
www.roksandailincic.com

Canada
Milli
310 Main Street West
Hamilton ON L8P 1J8
1-888-527-1531
www.roksandailincic.com

The Room – Hudson Bay
176 Yonge Street
Toronto ON M5C 2L7
1-416-861-9111
www.roksandailincic.com

U.K.
Browns
23–27 South Moulton Street
London W1K 5RD
+44 (0) 20 7514 0016
www.roksandailincic.com

Flannels
Crown Square
Spinningfields
Manchester M3 3FL
+44 (0) 161 832 5536
www.roksandailincic.com

68–78 Vicar Lane
Leeds LS1 7JH
+44 (0) 113 234 9977
www.roksandailincic.com

Australia
Cactus Jam
729 Glenferrie Road
Hawthorn VIC 3122
61-03-9819-0348
www.roksandailincic.com

Smythe
U.S.A.
Ooh La Shoppe
25 The Plaza
Locust Valley
New York NY 11560
1-516-801-2700
www.smythelesvestes.com

Ron Herman
325 North Beverly Drive
Beverly Hills CA 90210
1-310-550-0910
www.smythelesvestes.com

Saks Fifth Avenue
9600 Wilshire Boulevard
Beverly Hills CA 90212
1-310-275-4211
www.smythelesvestes.com

Canada
Coup Boutique
10137 104 Street Northwest
Edmonton AB T5J 0Z9
1-780-756-3032
www.smythelesvestes.com

Holt Renfrew
240 Sparks Street
Ottawa ON K1P 6C9
1-613-238-2200
www.smythelesvestes.com

Ssense
90 Rue Saint Paul Ouest
Montreal QC H2Y 3S5
1-514-289-1906
www.smythelesvestes.com

U.K.
Square One
43 St Johns Wood
London NW8 7NJ
+44 (0) 20 7586 8658
www.smythelesvestes.com

Trilogy
33 Duke of York Square
London SW3 4LY
+44 (0) 20 7730 6515
www.smythelesvestes.com

Rocca Boutique
32 Montpellier Parade
Harrogate
North Yorkshire HG1 2TG
+44 (0) 1423 564146
www.smythelesvestes.com

Stella McCartney
U.S.A.
112 Greene Street
New York NY 10014
1-212-255-1556
www.stellamccartney.com

Saks Fifth Avenue
9600 Wilshire Boulevard
Beverly Hills CA 90212
1-310-275-4211
www.stellamccartney.com

Saks Fifth Avenue
5800 Glades Road
Boca Raton FL 33431
1-561-393-9100
www.stellamccartney.com

U.K.
30 Bruton Street
London W1J 6QR
+44 (0) 20 7518 3100
www.stellamccartney.com

91–95 Fulham Road
London SW3 6RH
+44 (0) 20 7589 0092
www.stellamccartney.com

Selfridges
400 Oxford Street
London W1A 1AB
+44 (0) 20 7318 2326
www.stellamccartney.com

Temperley London
U.S.A.
8452 Melrose Place
West Hollywood CA 90069
1-323-782-8000
www.temperleylondon.com

U.K.
27 Bruton Street
London W1J 6QN
+44 (0) 20 7229 7957
www.temperleylondon.com

2–10 Colville Mews
Lonsdale Road
London W11 2DA
+44 (0) 20 7229 7957
www.temperleylondon.com

Topshop
U.S.A.
830 North Michigan Avenue
Chicago 60611
1-312-280-6834
www.topshop.com

3200 Las Vegas Boulevard South
Las Vegas NV 89109
1-702-866-0646
www.topshop.com

478 Broadway
New York NY 10013
1-212-966-9555
www.topshop.com

Canada
Topshop, Pacific Centre
674 Granville Street
Vancouver BC V6C 1Z6
1-604-681-6211
www.topshop.com

U.K.
Brigstowe Street
Bristol BS1 3BA
+44 (0) 117 9294991
www.topshop.com

65–67 New Street
Huddersfield HD1 2BQ
+44 (0) 1484 517149
www.topshop.com

36–38 Great Castle Street
London W1W 8LG
020 7927 7643
www.topshop.com

Australia
500 Chapel Street
South Yarra VIC 3141
61-3-8844-0900
www.topshop.com

Twenty8Twelve
U.K.
8 Slingsby Place
London WC2E 9AB
+44 (0) 20 7042 3500
www.twenty8twelve.com

172 Westbourne Grove
London W11 2RW
+44 (0) 20 7221 9287
www.twenty8twelve.com

Westfield
London W12 7GF
+44 (0) 20 8749 2450
www.twenty8twelve.com

Westfield Stratford City
London E20 1EN
+44 (0) 20 8221 1724
www.twenty8twelve.com

Warehouse
U.K.
19–21 Argyll Street
London W1F 7TR
+44 (0) 20 7437 7101
www.warehouse.co.uk

House of Fraser
45–51 Park Street
Camberley
Surrey GU15 3PG
+44 (0) 1276 418 050
www.warehouse.co.uk

Selfridges
400 Oxford Street
London W1A 1AB
+44 (0) 113 369 8040
www.warehouse.co.uk

Whistles
U.K.
135–136 Upper Street
London N1 1QP
+44 (0) 20 7226 7551
www.whistles.co.uk

3–7 Middle Pavement
Nottingham NG1 7DX
+44 (0) 11594 75551
www.whistles.co.uk

John Lewis
10 Downing Street
Cambridge CB2 3DS
+44 (0) 1223 361292
www.whistles.co.uk

John Lewis Oxford Street
278–306 Oxford Street
London W1C 1DX
+44 (0) 20 7629 7711
www.whistles.co.uk

Zara
U.S.A.
212 Newbury Street
Boston MA 02116
1-617-236-1414
www.zara.com

6902 Hollywood Blvd.
Los Angeles CA 90028
1-323-469-1002
www.zara.com

689 5th Ave
New York NY 10022
1-212-371-2555
www.zara.com

Canada
Chinook Centre
6455 MacLeod Trail SW
Calgary AB T2H OK8
1-403-538-2357
www.zara.com

U.K.
118 Regent Street
London W1B 5FE
+44 (0) 20 7534 9500
www.zara.com

79–83 Brompton Road
London SW3 1DB
+44 (0) 20 7590 6960
www.zara.com

48–52 Kensington High Street
London W8 4PE
+44 (0) 20 7368 4680
www.zara.com

Australia
Bourke Street Mall
Melbourne VIC
03-8663-0400
www.zara.com

Westfield Sydney
Sydney NSW
02-9216-7000
www.zara.com

Hair

**James Pryce and Richard Ward
at Richard Ward salon**
U.S.A.
Yarok Beauty Kitchen
39 West 19th Street
New York 10011
1-212-876-4293
www.yarokhair.com

U.K.
82 Duke of York Square
London SW3 4LY
+44 (0) 20 7730 1222
http://richardward.com

Jewelry

Annoushka
U.K.
41 Cadogan Gardens
London SW3 2TB
+44 (0) 20 7881 5828
www.annoushka-jewellery.com

1 South Molton Street
London W1K 5QF
+44 (0) 20 7629 8233
www.annoushka-jewellery.com

Bicester Village
50 Pingle Drive
Oxon OX26 6WD
+44 (0) 186 924 9948
www.annoushka-jewellery.com

Azuni
U.K.
John Lewis
300 Oxford Street
London W1A 1EX
+44 (0) 20 7629 7711
http://azuni.co.uk

Buckley (Adrian Buckley)
U.K.
www.buckleylondon.com

Cartier
U.S.A.
653 Fifth Avenue
New York NY 10022
1-212-753-0111
www.cartier.co.uk

Eyes on Lincoln
708 Lincoln Road
Miami Beach FL 33139
1-305-532-0070
www.cartier.co.uk

Saks Fifth Avenue
310 Canal Street
New Orleans LA 70130
1-504-524-2200
www.cartier.co.uk

Canada
3401 Dufferin Street
Toronto ON M6A 2T9
1-416-787-7474
www.cartier.co.uk

U.K.
143–144 Sloane Street
London SW1X 9AY
+44 (0) 20 7312 6930
www.cartier.co.uk

40–41 Old Bond Street
London W1S 4QR
+44 (0) 20 7290 5150
www.cartier.co.uk

Selfridges
400 Oxford Street
London W1A 1AB
+44 (0) 20 7318 3977
www.cartier.co.uk

Australia
The Moroccan Center
9–11 Elkhorn Avenue
Surfers Paradise
1800-13-0000
www.cartier.co.uk

43 Castlereagh Street
Sydney NSW
1800-13-0000
www.cartier.co.uk

Catherine Zoraida
U.K.
Austique
330 King's Road
London SW3 5UR
+44 (0) 20 7376 4555
www.catherinezoraida.com

Felt
13 Cale Street
London SW3 3QS
+44 (0) 20 7349 8829
www.catherinezoraida.com

Wolf & Badger
46 Ledbury Road
London W11 2AB
+44 (0) 20 7229 5698
www.catherinezoraida.com

Garrard
U.S.A.
Saks Fifth Avenue
384 Post Street
San Francisco CA 94108
1-415-986-4300
www.garrard.com

V.A.U.L.T
1024 Lincoln Road
Miami Beach FLA 33139
1-305-673-5251
www.garrard.com

U.K.
24 Albemarle Street
London W1S 4HT
www.garrard.com

Harvey Nichols
109–125 Knightsbridge
London SW1X 7RJ
+44 (0) 20 7235 5000
www.garrard.com

Heavenly Necklaces
U.K.
+44 (0) 203 162 3048
www.heavenlynecklaces.com

Kiki McDonough (see
Accessories, page 165)

Links of London
U.S.A.
The Mall at Short Hills
115 Short Hills NJ 07078
1-973-376-0911
www.linksoflondon.com

535 Madison Avenue
New York 10022
1-212-588-1177
www.linksoflondon.com

Links of London at Bloomingdales
909 North Michigan Avenue
Chicago IL 60611
1-312-440-4460
www.linksoflondon.com

Canada
Holt Renfrew
Eaton Centre
Calgary T2P 4H9
1-403-269-7341
www.linksoflondon.com

Holt Renfrew
10180 101 Street Northwest
Edmonton AB T5J 3S4
1-780-425-5300
www.linksoflondon.com

Holt Renfrew
Bloor Street
Toronto M4W 1A1
1-416-960-4039
www.linksoflondon.com

U.K.
Fenwick
Brent Cross Shopping Centre
London NW4 3FN
+44 (0) 20 8732 8285
www.linksoflondon.com

94 Jermyn Street
London SW1Y 6JE
+44 (0) 20 7930 0400/0401
www.linksoflondon.com

Westfield
London W12 7GD
+44 (0) 20 8749 7774
www.linksoflondon.com

Tiffany & Co. (Elsa Peretti)
U.S.A.
730 North Michigan Avenue
Chicago, IL 60611
1-312-944-7500
www.tiffany.com

Fifth Avenue and 57th Street
New York, NY 10022
1-212-755-8000
www.tiffany.com

5481 Wisconsin Avenue
Chevy Chase, MD 20815
1-301-657-8777
www.tiffany.com

Canada
25 The West Mall
Toronto, ON M9C 1B8
1-416-695-2112
www.tiffany.ca

3401 Dufferin Street
Toronto, Ontario M6A 2T9
1-416-780-6570
www.tiffany.ca

37 Dunsmuir Street
Vancouver BC V7Y 1E4
1-604-235-4111
www.tiffany.ca

U.K.
25 Old Bond Street
London W1S 4QB
+44 (0) 20 7409 2790
www.tiffany.co.uk

145 Sloane Street
London SW1X 9AY
+44 (0) 20 7409 2790
www.tiffany.co.uk

Westfield
London W12 7GQ
+44 (0) 20 7409 2790
www.tiffany.co.uk

Australia
226 Queen Street
Brisbane, QLD 4000
1-800-731-131
www.tiffany.com.au

37 King Street
Perth WA 6000
1-800-731-131
www.tiffany.com.au

28 Castlereagh Street
Sydney NSW 2000
1-800-731-131
www.tiffany.com.au

Makeup & Fragrances

Bobbi Brown
U.S.A.
Bobbi Brown – The Studio
8 Lackawanna Plaza
Montclair, NJ 07042
1-973-783-3506
www.bobbibrowncosmetics.com

Dillard's
6000 West Markham
Little Rock AR 72205
1-501-661-0053
www.bobbibrowncosmetics.com

Sephora
150 Broadway
New York NY 10038
1-212-566-8600
www.bobbibrowncosmetics.com

Cosmetic World
3250 West Olympic Blvd.
Los Angeles CA 90006
1-323-734-0777
www.bobbibrowncosmetics.com

Index

Figures in italics indicate captions.

Acknowledgments

The publishers would like to thank the following sources for their kind permission to reproduce the pictures in this book.
Key: t=Top, b=Bottom, c=Center, l=Left and r=Right
Annoushka Jewellery: 118cr, 163 (Pearl earring drops)
Anya Hindmarch: 38r, 163c (Black silk "Maud" clutch)
Bear Holding Ltd: 71
Beulah London: www.beulahlondon.com: 127
Catherine Zoraida: www.catherinezoraida.com: 130r, 163c ("Spread Your Wings" gold bracelet)
Corbis: Mike Nelson/epa: 7
Images Courtesy East Anglia's Children's Hospices: 79t, 79b,163c (Bracelet: The EACH Bracelet, exclusively designed by Imogen Sheeran, is available to buy online at www.each.org.uk/bracelet)
Emmy Shoes: www.emmyshoes.co.uk: 83r
Getty Images: 1, 4, 9, 11, 23br, 25r, 29br, 33br, 34, 47, 48t, 51r, 52, 65b, 66, 67, 94, 95l, 96, 98, 100, 101r, 102, 103, 110, 111tr, 117b, 117b, 133, 134r, 135, 136, 137, 144, 144b, 148, 149, 150tr, 150bl, 150br, 153, 160bl, 164, 2011 100 Women In Hedge Funds: 80, 2012 Indigo: 88t, AFP: 14, 23tl, 23tr, 39, 41tr, 45l, 45r, 72l, 74, 75, 77, 84, 106, 113, 123l, 125, 138, 140, FilmMagic: 20–21, 72br, UK Press: 10l, 19, 89, 146l, 152, 160tc, WireImage: 29tl, 29tcl, 29bc, 29bcr, 33l, 33tr, 36tr, 36br, 37, 41l, 44, 46, 48b, 49, 54l, 54r, 58, 65c, 78, 120l, 120r, 123r, 142, 146r, 161, 163c (Red hat)
Heavenly Necklaces: 101l, 162tl
Jimmy Choo: 57, 63, 131l, 162cl, 162br
Kiki McDonough: 59tr, 68r, 115, 163c (Citrine drop earrings, Blue topaz and diamond earrings & White topaz and diamond stud earrings)
L.K. Bennett: 55, 163c ("Natalie" natural clutch)
Libélula: 88c, 91
Next Plc: 76
Press Association Images: Lefteris Pitarakus/PA Archive: 61
Profile: Illuminum: 40
R. Soles: 50r, 163c (Vegas Setter boots)
Reiss: 35
Rex Features: 10r, 12, 15, 16, 17, 18, 23tc, 23bl, 26–27, 38l, 50l, 62, 64, 85l, 87, 92, 95r, 114, 131tr, 131br, 134l, 147, 154, 156, 163l, Ben Cawthra: 97l, 97tr, 97br, 99, Malcolm Clarke/Daily Mail: 22r, Davidson/O'Neill: 8, Paul Grover: 104, 158, David Hartley/Rupert Hartley: 68l, 69t, 83l, 85r, 86br, 163r, Ikon Pictures/Niraj Tanna: 90, Nils Jorgensen: 72tr, 159, Keystone USA-Zuma: 43, 51l, Eddie Mulholland: 150tl, NTI Media Ltd: 70, Newspix: 141, Niviere-Chamussy/Sipa: 107, 108, 109, Dominic O'Neill: 24l, Tim Rooke: 24r, 56, 59tl, 59b, 60, 65t, 81, 86tl, 86tr, 86bl, 112, 116, 119, 121, 122, 126, 129, 130l, Rotello/MCP: 13, Richard Young: 29tr, 82
Russell & Bromley: 69b, 111br, 118tl, 118br, 162bl,163c ("Park Avenue" clutch bag and matching shoes)
Séraphine: 160tl, 160r,160cb
Stuart Weitzman: 86b, 111bl, 163c, ("Coco Pop" navy shoes)

Every effort has been made to acknowledge correctly and contact the source and/or copyright holder of each picture and Carlton Books Limited apologizes for any unintentional errors or omissions, which will be corrected in future editions of this book.